INSIGHT POCKET GUIDES

# Israel

APA PUBLICATIONS
Part of the Langenscheidt Publishing Group

Israel
30 km / 19 miles
Mediterranean Sea
LEBANON
SYRIA
JORDAN
EGYPT
ISRAEL
WEST BANK
GAZA
Sur (Tyre)
Metula
Hermon
Majdal e-Shams
Kiryat Shmona
Buq'ata
Hula Valley
GOLAN HEIGHTS
Kuneitra (Qunaitra)
As Samnama
Kfar Rosh ha-Nikra
Nahariya
Mi'ilya
Meron Mts
Rehaniya
Akko (Acre)
Rama
Safed
Katsrin
Karmi'el
Kiryat Yam
Sea of Galilee (Yam Kinneret)
Israeli Disengagement Line
Syrian Disengagement Line
Izra
HAIFA (HEFA)
Shfar'am
Kiryat Tiv'on
Tiberias (Tverya)
Mt Carmel
Jezreel Valley
Nazareth (Natsarat)
Atlit
Um Qeis
Deraa
Zikhron Ya'akov
Megiddo
Afula
Irbid
Ramtha
Beit She'an
Khadera
Jenin
Samu'a
Araba
Mafraq
Netanya
Tul Karm
Sebastya
Tubas
Anjara
Kalkilya (Qalqilya)
Jordan (Yarden)
Kuraime
Jarash
Ra'anana
Nablus (Shkhem)
Herzliya
Kfar Saba
Hares
Mut'halat el-Misri
Abu Nuseir
TEL AVIV-YAFO (TEL AVIV-JAFFA)
Petakh Tikva
Bat Yam
Salt
Suweileh
Zarqa
Wadi e-Sir
Rishon Le-Tsiyon
Lod
El-Bira
AMMAN
Nes Tsiyona
Ramla
Jericho (Yerikho)
Yavne
Rekhovot
Ramalla
Na'ur
Ashdod
Gedera
Abu Ghosh
Moab Mts
Muwaqqar
JERUSALEM (YERUSHALAYIM)
Kiryat Mal'akhi
Beit Shemesh
Madaba
Jiza
Ashkelon
Bethlehem (Beit Lekhem)
Ma'in
Kiryat Gat
Beit Awla
Dead Sea (Yam ha-Melah)
Beit Lahiya
Beit Hanun
Halhul
Lib
Gaza
Sderot
Hebron (Khevron, El Khalil)
Nuseirat
Yata (Yuta)
Ein Gedi
Deir el-Balah
Netivot
Khan Yunis
Rahat
Samu'a
Tse'elim
Qasr
Rafah (Rafi'akh)
Ofakim
Meitar
Bab edh-Dhra
Arad
Tarsag
Be'er Sheva
Kseifa
Qatrana
El'Arîsh
Karak
Aro'er
Khalutsa Sands
Dimona
Mazar
Menzil
Yerukham
Risân 'Aneiza 368
Wadi el 'Arish
Kmehin
Ne'ot ha-Kikar
Safi
Sde Boker
Negev (Ha-Negev)
Tafila
Hesa
Ein Khatseva
J. Halâl 892
El Quseima
Ein-Yahav
Dana
Jurf ed-Darvis
Mitspe Ramon
Makhtesh Ramon
Tsofar
H. Harif 1000
Bîr Hasana
Shobed
J. Yi'allaq 1094
Paran
Abu Jirdhan
Jafr
Ayl
Maan
Gharandal
Ne'ot Smadar (Shizafon)
Ras en-Naqb
El Kutilla
Nakhl
Sinai
Yotvata
Ha-Arava
Elifaz
Quweira
Rum
El Thamad
Eilat
Jebel el Tîh
Gulf of Eilat
Aqaba

# Welcome!

Whether it's as the Holy Land or as one of the world's most stubborn trouble spots, Israel is regularly in the media spotlight. But the country is so much more than the sum of its religious history and contemporary politics. Israelis themselves are often more concerned with the fortunes of local soccer teams Maccabi Haifa and Betar Jerusalem or the performance of the Tel Aviv stock exchange than they are with the Arab-Israeli divide. And visitors who come on a pilgrimage are delighted to find glorious beaches and a vibrant city life as well as holy sites.

In these pages Insight's correspondent in Israel, Simon Griver, helps visitors get the most out of Israel during a short stay of a week or two. Splitting the country into five key bases – Jerusalem, Galilee, Haifa, Tel Aviv and Eilat – he has created a series of itineraries linking the country's main sights as well as less obvious attractions that only someone intimately acquainted with Israel is likely to know. Supporting the itineraries are sections on history and culture, shopping, eating out and nightlife as well as a practical information section that includes a list of recommended hotels.

Though born and brought up in Great Britain, **Simon Griver** has lived in Israel since 1978, where he works as a freelance journalist regularly contributing features on Israel to journals worldwide. 'Even after living in the country so long,' says Simon, 'the year-round sunshine, the exotic desert landscapes and the informality of the people give me the feeling of being permanently on holiday, even when I have the most hectic of work schedules.'

## C O N T E N T S

### History & Culture

### Israel's Highlights

**These 12 itineraries link the highlights of Israel. They divide into five key areas – Jerusalem and surroundings (1–5), Galilee (6 and 7), Haifa (8 and 9), Tel Aviv (10 and 11) and Eilat (12).**

*Pages 2/3: View from Mount Scopus*

#### JERUSALEM

#### GALILEE

*Pages 8/9: view of Jerusalem*

# HISTORY & CULTURE

Israel is a fascinating fusion of East and West, ancient and modern, sacred and profane. It has golden, sun-soaked beaches and stunningly beautiful landscapes, but above all else it is the Holy Land where Solomon built his Temple, Christ preached his sermons and from where Mohammed ascended to heaven. Even the visitor who remains unmoved by the religious significance of Israel is bound to be impressed by its rich archaeological and historical heritage reaching back to the dawn of civilisation.

## The Old Testament and Before

The history of the region begins long before biblical times. Jewellery and agricultural implements discovered in caves on Mount Carmel date back 12,000 years, while the 9,000-year-old fortifications at Jericho are the most ancient evidence of human civilisation. As Egypt and Mesopotamia emerged as mighty kingdoms some 5,000 years ago, Canaanite tribes founded city-kingdoms based on trade between the two neighbouring powers.

About 4,000 years ago, Abraham, the son of a Mesopotamian merchant, travelled westwards to Be'er Sheva. According to the Book of Genesis, he was the first man to recognise a single deity. His son Ishmael was to father the Arab-Islamic heritage, while from his second son, Isaac, and Isaac's son Jacob, Judaeo-Christian civilisation springs. Jacob had 12 sons, among whom the favourite, Joseph, was sold into slavery in Egypt by his jealous brothers.

*Camels in the Judean desert*

Joseph prospered in Egypt and was joined there by his family. The Book of Exodus relates how generations later the Children of Israel were enslaved by the Egyptians before being led out of bondage by Moses and back to the Promised Land where they defeated Canaanite tribes and settled the inland hills, while the coastal plain remained in the hands of the Philistines to the south and the Phoenicians to the north.

*Map of the Land of Canaan*

At first ruled by warrior judges such as Samuel, the Children of Israel looked for a king who could unite the tribes. Saul assumed the crown and paved the way for a golden era beginning under his successor David, who moved his capital from Hebron to a nearby Jebusite hilltop settlement that he captured and called Jerusalem. David, a soldier and poet, transformed Israel into a prosperous kingdom, extending its borders to Syria in the north and the Red Sea in the south.

Solomon consolidated his father's military achievements and developed the kingdom's new capital, Jerusalem, by building the Temple, to house the Ark of the Covenant, said to contain the tablets of the Ten Commandments given to Moses by God on Mount Sinai. But despite his wisdom Solomon left no obvious heir and squabbles among his successors resulted in the division of the kingdom. Ten of the tribes established the kingdom of Israel in the north, while the state of Judah encompassed the tribe of Benjamin.

Division resulted in decline. By 722BC the northern kingdom was defeated by the Assyrians who exiled the 10 tribes. Their unknown fate remains a mystery today though many peoples worldwide claim tenuous descent from the 'ten lost tribes'. Judah, however, accepted Assyrian sovereignty for a further 150 years before the Babylonian leader Nebuchadnezzar, as the Book of Ezekiel tells us, captured Jerusalem, destroyed the Temple and exiled the Jews to Babylon.

The exile lasted 40 years until the Persians conquered Babylon and

*Third-century boat*

*Byzantine tomb decoration*

allowed the Jews to return to Jerusalem and rebuild the Temple. Two centuries of Persian rule were followed by two centuries of Greek hegemony. Peace prevailed until the Greeks attempted to impose idolatry. In 164BC the Hasmonean family led a successful insurrection against the Greeks and restored Jewish sovereignty. Independence lasted for a century, until the Roman conquest in 63BC.

## The Advent of Christianity

The Romans allowed Judea, the Latin name for the region, to be ruled by autonomous Jewish kings. The most notorious of these was Herod the Great, whose reign lasted from 37–4BC. Remembered as a bloodthirsty leader, he also completed grandiose projects such as a new capital at Caesarea on the Mediterranean coast. As popular dissatisfaction grew against the government, the time was ripe for a messianic saviour.

*Roman mosaic*

Christ had a limited impact during his own lifetime. The historian Josephus makes reference to a Galilean preacher who was eventually crucified by the Romans. But Christ was surrounded by a dedicated group of disciples who spread his teachings after his death. Indeed, the years following Christ's death were tumultuous, culminating in a Jewish uprising when the Romans placed an image of the Emperor Caligula in the Temple.

The rebellion was quickly quelled, except in Jerusalem which held out under siege for three years. When the Romans retook the city, they destroyed the Temple. Only the Western Wall of the Temple complex was left standing; it remains today the holiest shrine in Judaism. Other Jewish hilltop fortresses such as Masada, near the Dead Sea, resisted for several more years before they were crushed by the military might of Rome (*see pages 41–42*).

*Qumran: site of the Dead Sea Scrolls*

A ceasefire held until AD132 when a Jewish revolt was mercilessly quashed. The Jewish leaders were executed or exiled and Jerusalem was renamed Aeolina Capitolina. From this date the Jewish people consider that the exile began. Nevertheless, communities of Jewish scholars flourished in the Galilee for several centuries, penning the Talmud, the compendium of Jewish commentary and the mystical texts of the Kabbalah.

Christianity took hold in the Holy Land following the conversion of the Roman Emperor Constantine in the 4th century. He despatched his mother, Queen Helena, from Byzantium to identify sites associated with Christ's life. Chapels were constructed at these places in Bethlehem, Jerusalem and the Galilee. Larger churches have since been added and these locations remain the focus of Christian pilgrimages today.

## The Rise of Islam

By the 5th century Christians formed a majority in Palestine. This situation prevailed until the Arab-Muslim conquest of Jerusalem in 640, after which most of the local population converted to Islam. In 691 Caliph Abd Al-Malik constructed the Dome of the Rock on the Temple Mount over the spot where Muslims believe Mohammed ascended to heaven. Several decades later the silver-domed El Aqsa Mosque was also built on the Temple Mount.

Islamic hegemony was rudely interrupted by the Crusaders, who in 1099 established the Kingdom of Jerusalem to control the Holy Land. The Crusaders viewed all non-Catholics as infidels, and indigenous Muslims, Christians and Jews alike were slaughtered. The Crusaders dominated the region for 150 years and built hilltop fortresses whose ruins can still be seen today. Crusader power waned in 1187 after a victory by the Egyptian leader Saladin, and the last European stronghold in Acco (Acre) fell in 1291.

*Tel Aviv from Jaffa mosque*

The Mamelukes, Asiatic slave warriors who had conquered Egypt, ruled the region for over two centuries and this was a period of decline for Palestine. In 1492 Jewish communities were re-established in Jerusalem and the Galilee following the expulsion of Jews from Spain, and in 1516 the Ottoman Turks seized control of the Holy Land. While the Ottomans prospered so did Palestine, and during the 16th century Suleiman the Magnificent built the walls around Jerusalem. But by the 17th century the Ottoman Empire was in decline and Palestine entered a long period of stagnation.

*Soldiers on guard*

## The Emergence of Zionism

The 19th century saw a renewal of interest in Palestine. The European imperialistic powers, especially Britain and France, vied for influence in the Holy Land. More significantly, rising anti-Semitism in Europe compelled Jews to reconsider their identity. Emigration to Israel began as a trickle: Jewish philanthropists built suburbs in Jerusalem and north of Jaffa, and agricultural settlements were set up for Jews from the Russian Empire.

The Zionist movement was established in 1897 when an Austrian-Jewish journalist, Theodore Herzl, covering the trial of the framed French-Jewish officer Albert Dreyfus in Paris, concluded that anti-Semitism was intrinsically rooted in European culture. By the early 20th century, the Zionist movement was taken over by Jewish so-

*Praying at the Western Wall*

*Independence Day fervour*

cialists escaping the upheaval of pre-revolutionary Russia. The British defeat of the Ottomans in 1917 and the declaration by Britain's Foreign Minister, Lord Balfour, that his government backed the establishment of a Jewish homeland in Palestine gave Zionism international legitimacy.

The Palestinian Arab population reacted violently and Jews were massacred throughout the 1920s. But Arab opposition did not stop Jewish immigration. After World War I, Europe was in turmoil and, with anti-Semitism escalating, more Jews set out for Palestine. Under the leadership of a young Russian socialist, David Ben Gurion, the Jews organised militarily and economically. Tel Aviv grew into a fashionable city, while kibbutzim, socialist agricultural collectives, produced food. By 1930 the Jewish population of Palestine numbered 120,000.

Faced with Arab hostility, the British changed course. All Palestine east of the River Jordan was ceded to the Hashemite tribe of Saudi Arabia in 1923 and eventually became Jordan. Following the rise of Nazism in Germany, and expectations of mass Jewish emigration from Europe, the British limited Jewish entry into Palestine.

*A Jewish wedding*

## The Establishment of Israel

The discovery of the Nazi death camps and the extermination of six million European Jews created a climate of international sympathy for the Zionist cause, but this was not reflected in British policy. Britain, and initially the United States, opposed the partition of Palestine into Jewish and Arab states. Then a militant bombing campaign against British targets by right-wing Zionist groups persuaded the British government to hand the issue over to the United Nations and set a date for troop withdrawal.

Shrewd Jewish lobbying in the US combined with the support of Soviet dictator Josef Stalin, who saw a Jewish state as a socialist bulwark against European imperialism, secured a majority in the UN for the partition of Palestine. In May 1948 Ben Gurion declared Israel an independent state. The new state was immediately attacked by its Arab neighbours and, in the War of Independence, Israel won parts of the Galilee and Negev allocated by the UN to the Arabs. Jerusalem was divided, with Jordan occupying the eastern half of the city and the West Bank,

*Old men in the Old City*

while Egypt seized Gaza. This status quo remained until 1967 when, during the Six Day War, Israel captured East Jerusalem, the West Bank and Gaza as well as the Sinai from Egypt and the Golan Heights from Syria.

Sinai was returned to Egypt following a peace treaty in 1979, while the Oslo Accords in 1993 saw Israel grant autonomy to most of the Gaza Strip and the main cities of the West Bank. A final status settlement with the Palestinians was on the agenda. But, in the wake of a Hamas bombing campaign and the victory of Binyamin Netanyahu's right-wing government in 1996, progress slowed.

Despite the Israeli–Arab conflict, Israel's accomplishments have been remarkable. With a population of nearly 6 million, including a 20 percent Arab minority and Jewish immigrants from every continent, Israel has remained a parliamentary democracy. The assassination of Prime Minister Yitzhak Rabin in 1995 served only to show that democracy has deep roots in Israel. His deputy, Shimon Peres, assumed the premiership, although he was defeated soon after at the polls.

Though divided between orthodox and secular, Western Ashkenazi and Oriental Sephardi Jews, left and right, veterans and newcomers, the country maintains a cohesive, dynamic culture glued together by Hebrew, the language of the Bible resurrected for modern use. Despite wars and mass immigration, the economy is flourishing and the country enjoys a standard of living comparable to parts of Western Europe.

*'King David' takes to the streets*

Israelis themselves are a diverse, dynamic, informal and argumentative people. Beneath their often abrasive surface, they can be refreshingly open and have a sense of hospitality and communicativeness that can make a visit to Israel unforgettable.

## Historical Highlights

**10,000BC–6,000BC** Inhabitants settle the Jordan Valley and Mediterranean coast.

**3,000BC** Canaanite city kingdoms develop.

**c2,000BC** Abraham settles in Be'er Sheva.

**c1,280BC** Moses leads Israelites out of Egypt.

**c1,000BC** King David decides on Jerusalem as his capital.

**c950BC** King Solomon builds the First Temple.

**586BC** The First Temple is destroyed and the Babylonian exile begins.

**546BC** Jews return to Jerusalem and build the Second Temple.

**333BC** Greeks conquer Jerusalem but allow Jews freedom of worship.

**164BC** Successful Jewish uprising after Greeks defile Temple.

**63BC** The Romans conquer Judea.

**37BC** King Herod assumes the throne.

**AD30** Crucifixion of Christ.

**66** Jews revolt against Rome.

**70** Romans recapture Jerusalem and destroy Temple.

**132** Revolt against Rome fails and Jews go into exile.

**325** Constantine converts to Christianity and despatches his mother to Palestine to identify sacred sites.

**638** Muslim conquest of Jerusalem.

**691** The Dome of the Rock is built on Temple Mount.

**1099** The Crusaders establish the Kingdom of Jerusalem.

**1187** Saladin defeats Crusaders.

**1291** Crusader stronghold in Akko (Acre) falls as the Mamelukes capture Palestine.

**1516** Ottomans capture Palestine.

**1541** Suleiman the Magnificent completes Jerusalem's walls.

**1881** Growing anti-Semitism in Russia forces many Jews to emigrate.

**1897** Theodore Herzl convenes first Zionist Congress.

**1917** British capture Palestine and voice support for the creation of a Jewish homeland.

**1920** Arab riots make British rethink policy.

**1925** Large-scale Jewish emigration from Central and Eastern Europe.

**1945** Horrors of the Holocaust become known. Survivors flock to Palestine but are imprisoned by British in Cyprus.

**1947** United Nations votes for partition of Palestine between a Jewish and an Atab state.

**1948** David Ben Gurion declares State of Israel.

**1949** War of Independence ends. Jordanians annex East Jerusalem and West Bank and Egypt takes the Gaza Strip.

**1956** Israel captures and returns Sinai following Suez campaign.

**1967** Israel captures East Jerusalem, West Bank, Gaza, Sinai and Golan Heights during the Six Day War.

**1973** Yom Kippur War.

**1977** Menachem Begin becomes Prime Minister for Likud, ending 29 years of Labour government.

**1979** An Israel–Egypt peace treaty is signed.

**1982** Israel invades Lebanon and the PLO is expelled to Tunisia.

**1987** Intifada begins.

**1991** Scud missiles fall on Israel during the Gulf War.

**1992** Yitzhak Rabin elected prime minister.

**1993** Agreement concluded in Oslo between Israel and PLO.

**1994** Israel signs peace agreement with Jordan.

**1995** Yitzhak Rabin assassinated by Jewish extremist. Shimon Peres becomes prime minister.

**1996** Binyamin Netanyahu elected prime minister.

**1997** Hebron is placed under Palestinian authority.

ROMEMA
Erets Khemda Institute
Israel TV (Channel 1)
KEREM AVRAHAM
Geological Institute
Shderot Weizman
Yirmiyahu
Shderot Sarei Yisra'el
Malkhei Yisra'el
Beit Miryam
Ha-Rav Kuk Institute
Yafo
ETS KHAYIM
MEKOR BARUKH
Merkaz ha-Rav Yeshiva
Shderot Shazar
Nordau
Yitskhak Ben Dor
MAKHANE YEHUDA
HA-MEKASHER
International Conference Centre (Binyanei ha-Uma)
Ministry of Foreign Affairs
Kiryat Moshe
Shderot Herzl
Beit ha-Khayal
Agripas
Ets Khayim Yeshiva
Ha-Nevi'im
Makhane Yehuda Market
Bikur Kholim Hospital
Beit Yad le-Baniem
NAKHLA'OT
KIRYAT BEN GURION
Theatre Museum
Gerard Bachar Centre
Bank of Israel
Wolfson
National Archives
Supreme Court
Ben Yehuda
Italian
Prime Minister Office
SACHER PARK
Betsal'el Academy
Ministry of the Interior
Ort College
Rubin Academy of Music
Science Museum
Derekh Ruppin
Rothschild
KIRYAT WOLFSON
Ratisbonne
Yeshurun
Sderot Ben Tsvi
Treasury
Grossberg Stadium
Knesset
The Jewish Agency
Beit ha-Sfarim ha-Le'umi (National Library)
Beit Belgia
Hebrew University
Bible Lands Museum
REKHAVYA
Heikhal Shlomo
Amphitheatre
NAVE SHA'ANAN
Shrine of the Book (Heikhal ha-Sefer)
Ramban
REKHAVYA PARK (VALLEY OF THE CROSS)
Jason's Tomb
Academy of Hebrew Language
Israel Museum
Cross
Sderot Khai'm Hazaz
KIRYAT SHMU'EL
Van Leer Foundation
NEVE GRANOT
Presidential Residence
Islamic Art
Jerusalem Centre of Performing Arts
David Marcus
Chopin
BOTANICAL GARDENS
NAYOT
Ha-Rav Herzog
Ha-Palmakh
Yad Va-Shem Holocaust Memorial & Museum
Betsal'el Bazak
SHIKUN RASKO
EMEK REFA'IM
Yeshivat Khevron
GONEN (KATAMON)
Rakhel Imenu

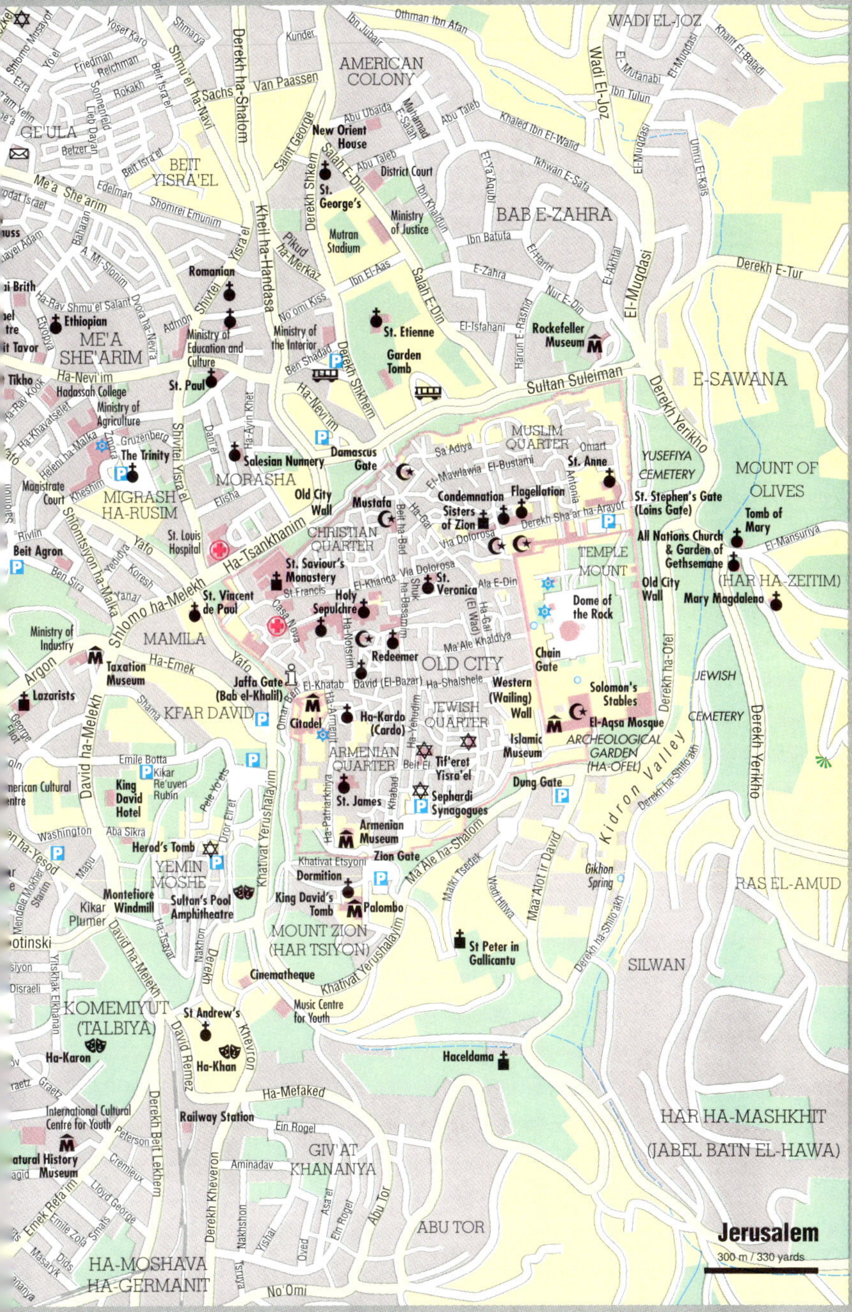
Jerusalem
300 m / 330 yards
OLD CITY
MUSLIM QUARTER
CHRISTIAN QUARTER
JEWISH QUARTER
ARMENIAN QUARTER
TEMPLE MOUNT
MOUNT OF OLIVES
(HAR HA-ZEITIM)
MOUNT ZION
(HAR TSIYON)
AMERICAN COLONY
BAB E-ZAHRA
E-SAWANA
WADI EL-JOZ
ME'A SHE'ARIM
GE'ULA
BEIT YISRA'EL
MORASHA
MIGRASH HA-RUSIM
MAMILA
KFAR DAVID
YEMIN MOSHE
KOMEMIYUT (TALBIYA)
GIV'AT KHANANYA
ABU TOR
HA-MOSHAVA HA-GERMANIT
SILWAN
RAS EL-AMUD
HAR HA-MASHKHIT
(JABEL BAT'N EL-HAWA)
Kidron Valley
Damascus Gate
Jaffa Gate (Bab el-Khalil)
Zion Gate
Dung Gate
St. Stephen's Gate (Loins Gate)
Dome of the Rock
El-Aqsa Mosque
Western (Wailing) Wall
Holy Sepulchre
Citadel
Rockefeller Museum
Garden Tomb
Tomb of Mary
All Nations Church & Garden of Gethsemane
King David's Tomb
Cinematheque
Railway Station

# Day Itineraries

Despite the high expectations that most visitors bring to Jerusalem, the Holy City does not disappoint. For believers, there are sites sacred to Jews, Christians and Muslims, but even for non-believers the city's remarkable history casts an enchanting spell. Situated at an elevation of over 800 metres (2,600ft) in the Judean Hills, Jerusalem overlooks forests to the west and desert to the east as well as the splendid panorama of the Old City.

The tourist sites – and much of the rest of the city – have been tastefully renovated and maintained, and the stone facades required by law give the city a timeless architectural homogeneity. Yet amid the history and religion, Jerusalem is a flourishing, vibrant place, the capital of modern Israel. It has a lively nightlife with restaurants and bars bustling with custom well into the small hours.

Though reunited politically in 1967, Jerusalem remains socially divided. Arab East Jerusalem is a world apart from Jewish West Jerusalem. West Jerusalem itself is deeply divided between ultra-orthodox Jewry and the rest of the Jewish community, both orthodox and secular.

The following five tours of the city and its surroundings assume that you are based in Jerusalem. No long journeys are necessary, though: Israel is a small country and it is less than a four-hour drive to Eilat in the south or the Golan Heights in the north.

*Resting outside Jaffa Gate*

# Jerusalem

## 1. The Old City

**A full day getting to know Jerusalem, including all the holy sites in the Old City. Following an afternoon rest, an evening in Me'a She'arim and a night on the town in West Jerusalem. This tour can only be done on foot, and modest dress for visiting the holy sites is compulsory. Non-Muslims are not admitted to the Temple Mount on Fridays or after midday, so plan accordingly.**

*–All sites are closed on Saturday. If you want to visit the Hasmonean Tunnel you must book in advance; tel: 02-6271333–*

*Jaffa Gate*

Enter the Old City by the **Jaffa Gate** (Sha'ar Yafo), which historically was the main entrance to Jerusalem because it faced the Mediterranean coast. Known in Arabic as Bab El Khalil (The Hebron Gate), its walls were breached and a roadway built a century ago so that Kaiser Wilhelm of Germany could enter on horseback. Immediately on your left is the **Tourist Information Centre** while facing you on the first street on the right is the **Christian Information Office**. On your right is the Tower of David.

Have a coffee at the Café St Michel on your left and savour the oriental atmosphere before descending into the labyrinthine bazaar. Then go straight on down through the Arab souk. Aggressively friendly shopkeepers will probably assault you with all manner of trinkets at 'special prices'. If you want to buy anything, be sure to bargain. The bustle, noise and potent smells of leather and spices are not for the claustrophobic.

At the end of the alleyway (El Bazar) just before a T-junction is a black sign overhead pointing right to the Kardo. Turn right here and almost immediately you leave the Muslim Quarter and enter the Jewish Quarter, re-built after its destruction by the Jordanians in 1948's War of Independence. After another few hundred metres you will enter the **Kardo**, the original Byzantine north–south road through Jerusalem which was unearthed when the quarter was being rebuilt; it is now a fashionable lane with expensive stores.

At the end of the Kardo climb the stairs to the left, go straight across into Beit El and turn left across the square and into Tiferet Yisrael. Go straight on and down the many steps of Yehuda Halevi to the Western Wall Plaza. The **Western Wall** is the only remaining structure from the Temple destroyed by the Romans in AD70. It had been built – by the poorest of Jews, it is said – to support the western portion of the Herodian Temple Mount, and these large blocks of stone now form the most important national symbol for the Jewish people. According to traditional Judaism, the Temple cannot be rebuilt until the Messiah comes, and the Diaspora Jews regard The Wall (or HaKotel) as their most sacred shrine. To pray here has been the abiding dream of observant Jews ever since the beginning of their exile 1,900 years ago.

*Western 'Wailing' Wall*

The Wall, which is as smooth as the endless stream of tears spilled mourning the destruction of the Temple, came to be known as the Wailing Wall. Anyone may approach it and lodge paper prayers in its cracks (its nickname is God's Letter-Box). You will note that women ('modestly dressed') enter on the left, men (heads covered) on the right. Men must also wear a *kippa* to cover the head (supplied at the entrance to the Wall). Photography is strictly forbidden on Shabbat (Saturday).

The Wall itself is 50ft (15 metres) tall, and most of the stones were carved and stacked here during Herod's time, but those at

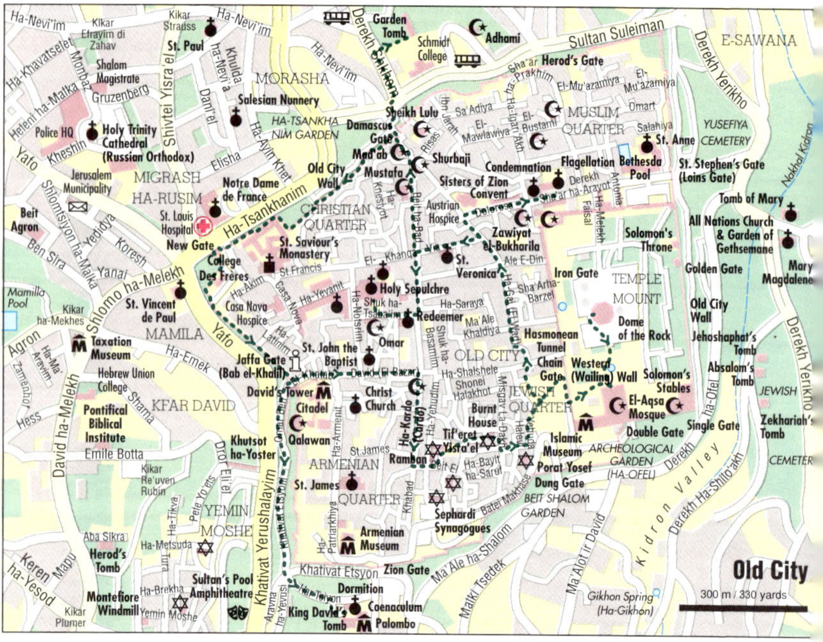

*Temple Mount steps*

and near the top were put there during restoration by the Mamelukes and Turks. When the Jordanian Legion captured the Old City in 1948, Jews were forbidden – as they had been many times throughout history – to worship at the Wall. So it was with special meaning, on 7 June 1967, that Jews everywhere watched TV footage of the Israeli Army retaking the Old City, and the young soldiers praying and weeping at the Wall.

Immediately following the Six Day War, the Arab shanties in the large area in front of the Wall were cleared, and the plaza was made into a place of worship. Traditionally, observant Jews gather here on holidays and days of mourning – especially on Tisha ba'Av, the anniversary of the Temple's destruction.

After leaving the Wall, turn left and left again up the narrow path and through the gateway to the **Temple Mount** (non-Muslims are not admitted after midday or on Fridays). Some orthodox Jews decline to enter the Temple Mount in case they inadvertently set foot on the Holy of Holies, the section of the Temple that only the High Priest could enter.

Temple Mount is a surprisingly large area, which indicates how vast the Temple must have been. According to tradition, this was Mount Moriah where, in the Book of Genesis, Abraham came to sacrifice Isaac. Immediately before you is the silver-domed El Aqsa Mosque and further over to your left the resplendent gold-roofed Dome of the Rock. There is a booth near the entrance to El Aqsa selling entry tickets to both buildings. When entering both El Aqsa and the Dome of the Rock, you must remove your shoes, according to Muslim custom.

**El Aqsa** was built in the 8th century. Unlike the Dome of the Rock, it is a mosque and, as such, is the most important Muslim place of worship in Jerusalem, and one of the most famous in the Islamic world. Non-Muslims are not permitted to enter the mosque during prayer. When you do go in, you have the feeling that you are walking into an elaborate carpet warehouse – the Persian rugs and lavish interior decorations have been contributed by countries all over the Muslim world.

The mosque is quite beautiful in its simplicity, and innovative for its use of six rows of columns set perpendicular to the wall which it is customary to face when one prays. Whereas Jews the world over face Jerusalem when they pray, Muslims face Mecca; in this case, that's toward the southern or back wall.

It was in front of El Aqsa in 1951 that a fanatic Muslim assassinated Jordan's King Abdullah in front of his grandson, the current King Hussein. In 1969, an Australian set the mosque aflame, provoking calls for a jihad against Israel. When Egypt's president,

*Dome of the Rock*

Anwar Sadat, visited in 1977, he came to pray at El Aqsa. There are still demonstrations there today, either by Palestinians trying to raise the national flag or by Israeli right-wingers. When the Crusaders conquered Jerusalem, they transformed El Aqsa into a royal palace before finally setting up the headquarters of the Order of the Knights of the Temple here – the Templars. It was recaptured for Islam by Saladin in 1187.

Built in AD691, the **Dome of the Rock**, to the north of El Aqsa, is one of the world's most resplendent buildings. The exterior is decorated in marble, painted tiles and stained glass in shades of blue, green and gold. In 1994 the Dome was re-covered with 25-carat gold provided by King Hussein of Jordan. The interior, with Persian rugs, is no less exquisite and beneath is the crypt containing the rock from where Mohammed is believed to have ascended to heaven on his horse after his death in Medina, and where Abraham attempted to sacrifice his son, as related in Genesis.

The Dome of the Rock, a shrine rather than a mosque, was built by the Caliph Abd al-Malik, who was horrified by the neglect of the Temple Mount. But it was Suleiman the Magnificent, in the 16th century, who refurbished the building in the highly aesthetic decorative style that we see today.

*The Islamic Museum*

Much to the chagrin of Jewish zealots the Temple Mount is completely in Muslim hands. Other attractions include a new mosque at Solomon's Stables in the southeastern corner and the **Islamic Museum** to the west of the El Aqsa mosque, which displays artefacts depicting Islamic life in Jerusalem. Entry to the museum is included in the price of the ticket for the Dome of the Rock and the El Aqsa mosque (Sunday to Thursday 8–11am and noon–3pm, closed Fridays and Muslim holidays).

Leave the Temple Mount via the same gate you entered and return to the Western Wall plaza. To the left of the Wall is the controversial **Hasmonean Tunnel**, a major thoroughfare in Roman times. The tunnel sparked major Arab riots when it was fully opened in 1996 (extreme Palestinian nationalists claimed groundlessly that it was a Zionist plot to excavate beneath the Temple Mount and blow up the mosques, though it had in fact already been open to the public as a cul-de-sac for nine years). A small entry fee is charged for entering the tunnel which skirts beneath the western perimeter of the Temple Mount.

The tunnel exits into the **Via Dolorosa** opposite the Franciscan sanctuary which includes the **Chapel of Condemnation** and the **Church of The Flagellation** at the **Second Station of the Cross**. This was where Christ was condemned and then flogged.

Otherwise you can get to the Via Dolorosa from the Western Wall by walking along Ha-Gai (El Wad) until you reach the Via Dolorosa at the Austrian Hospice. Turn right for about 300 metres and proceed until you reach the Churches of the Condemnation and Flagellation. (The **First Station of the Cross** is inside the Omariya School and inaccessible to the public.)

Now retrace your steps. A little way along Via Dolorosa is the Ecce Homo arch of the **Sisters of Zion Convent**. Enter on your right and go down to the cellars where the paving stones of the original Roman road, the 'Lithostrotos', are preserved. It is believed Christ passed along here as he bore the Cross.

The **Third Station**, outside the Armenian Patriarchate just before the Via Dolorosa meets up with Ha-Gai (El Wad), is unmarked. Turn left by the Austrian Hospice, an impressive 19th-century building, and make a right turn after about 100 metres at the Fifth Station. But, before you turn, note that on your left is Abu Shukri, a restaurant renowned for its excellent *hummus*, an ideal light lunch with pita bread.

Continuing along Via Dolorosa, the **Sixth Station**, where Veronica wiped Christ's face with a cloth, is on the left. Just before here is the **Karakashian Armenian Pottery Store** where tasteful gifts can be purchased. The **Seventh** and **Eighth stations** are each side of the junction with Souk Ha-Basamim (Souk Khan ez-Zeit), the main market thoroughfare, at which point the Via Dolorosa turns left. The **Ninth Station**, where Christ fell for the third time, is up the stairs on your right by the Coptic Orthodox Patriarchate, which is the entrance to the **Ethiopian Monastery** and the roof of the Holy Sepulchre. Along Souk Ha-Basamim, take the next alleyway to the right (Souk Ed

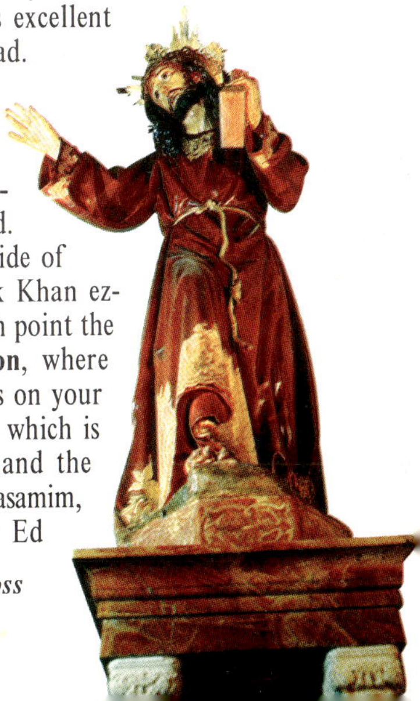

*Second Station of the Cross*

Dabbagha), and pass the **Church of the Redeemer**, a German Lutheran church whose spire is the tallest construction in the Old City. Now enter the compound of the Church of the Holy Sepulchre containing the remaining five stations of the Cross.

Constructed in 1149 by the Crusaders on the site of a Byzantine chapel, the **Church of the Holy Sepulchre** is jointly owned by the Catholics, Greek Orthodox, Ethiopian, Armenian and Coptic churches. Open every day from dawn until dusk the keys are held by a Muslim family and repairs are undertaken by the Israeli government to avoid proprietorial arguments. As you enter the church climb the steep stairway to the right. At the top, at the entrance to the right nave, is a Franciscan chapel containing the **Tenth** and **Eleventh** stations where Christ was stripped and nailed to the Cross. In the Greek Orthodox chapel to the left is the **Twelfth Station** where Christ was crucified, while the **Thirteenth Station**, where His body was handed to Mary, is back in the Franciscan Chapel. Back downstairs and past the front entrance you must queue and almost crawl through a short passage to the final **Fourteenth Station** – the tomb of Christ beneath a raised marble slab.

Return through the courtyard and back along to Souk Ha-Basamim (Souk Khan ez-Zeit). Turn left for the Arab market. This section has few souvenir shops and contains mainly food and clothing stores used by the locals. Connoisseurs may wish to hunt out a particular type of coffee or a rare spice. You will eventually reach **Damascus Gate**, the main entrance to the city for Arab Jerusalemites.

*The Garden Tomb*

After so much sightseeing, you may wish to return to your hotel for a rest before a night on the town. Alternatively if you still have the time, inclination and energy there is much to do and see. You may wish to visit the **Garden Tomb** (Monday to Saturday 8am–1pm and 3.30–5pm), which is several hundred metres ahead on the right-hand side of Derekh Shkhem (Nablus Road). Discovered in the 19th century by Britain's General Gordon, the Garden Tomb is regarded by some Protestants as the true site of the Holy Sepulchre. In any case, the gardens are an oasis of tranquillity offering a chance for meditation away from the hustle of the Old City.

Another option is to turn left outside the gate, go down the stairs beneath and back up to the **Ramparts Walk** (9am–4pm) along the top of the wall. Walk back round to Jaffa Gate and visit the **Citadel Museum of the History of Jerusalem** (Sunday to Thursday 10am–4pm and Friday to Saturday 10am–2pm) documenting the city's tumultuous history. Its displays include figurines of Jerusalem

*Orthodox communications*

characters, and the multi-layered ruins of the Citadel itself. A multimedia show with a separate entrance describes the city's various moods by means of numerous slide projectors. (The walls themselves are the palette for the sound and light show presented here in many languages most evenings from April to October.)

Outside Jaffa Gate you may wish to stroll along the beautiful parklands to Mount Zion where you can see **King David's Tomb** and the nearby **Coenaculum** where Christ supposedly ate the Last Supper. Or you may prefer to visit the Armenian Quarter (go back through Jaffa Gate and turn right), a walled ghetto within a walled city established 1,000 years ago by Armenian pilgrims.

Start your evening walk at the junction of **Shivtei Yisrael** and **Me'a She'arim**. Please take the warnings about modest attire seriously for the locals can be violent towards women showing too much flesh. Me'a She'arim is the main street of the quarter of the same name (meaning 'a hundred gates') which is a bastion of ultra-orthodox Judaism. The style of dress – *peot* (sidecurls), heavy black garments for the men and shawls for the women – derives from medieval Poland, and the surrounding streets, alleyways and courtyards typify Jewish life as it was in Eastern Europe several centuries ago.

Midway along Me'a She'arim turn left into Baharan and, leaving Me'a She'arim district, cross over into Etyopya Street, one of the city's most delightful and most expensive streets. On your left is the Ethiopian Church, built at the turn of the century. Cross over Ha-Nevi'im into Ha-Rav Kook. A little way down on your right is **Beit Tikho**, a pleasant garden café and restaurant occupying an 1860s house belonging to Anna Tikho, the city's foremost landscape artist, whose drawings are on display in the house.

Go to the bottom of Ha-Rav Kook where, a little to your left, is **Kikar Tsiyon** (Zion Square), the heart of downtown West Jerusalem. Stroll up and down **Ben Yehuda**, a pedestrian precinct containing inexpensive restaurants and cafés, or along the lanes of **Nahlat**

*Ben Yehuda at night*

**Yehuda**, such as Salomon and Rivlin, with their restaurants and souvenir shops. These streets are brimming with life until after midnight. A good restaurant to try for local delicacies is **Eucalyptus** in Horkanos which runs eastwards off Ha-Rav Kook.

After midnight the action shifts to the **Russian Compound**, an area acquired by Tsar Alexander II in 1853 as a refuge for the thousands of Russian pilgrims who flocked to the city every year. Near the Russian Orthodox Holy Trinity Cathedral, with its white walls and green domes, several dozen bars, which remain busy until nearly dawn, can be found on Mobaz and Heleni Ha-Malka streets.

## 2. Jerusalem Views and Bethlehem

**A day's drive in the region of Jerusalem, enjoying splendid views of the city and the surrounding desert from the Mount of Olives and Mount Scopus. Take in some culture at the Israel Museum and lunch at the Botanical Gardens. On to Bethlehem and the Church of the Nativity, and complete the day with some more breathtaking vistas from East Talpiyot. This tour must be done by car.**

Drive north of the city on Derekh ha-Shalom. Until 1967 the wall dividing the city between Israel and Jordan ran along this route. Turn right into Shderot ha-Universita ha-Ivrit (Hebrew University Boulevard) and left into Shderot Shayeret Har ha-Tsofim (Mount Scopus Boulevard) and right again into Shomrei ha-Har. You are now circling the campus of the Hebrew University (there are free tours in English). The university was founded here in 1926 but cut off from the rest of Israel from 1948 to 1967. To your right is a splendid view of the Old City. Napoleon once encamped near here but never tried to conquer the city. At the end of the road, stop again before turning right to take in the view of the Judean Desert and Jordan Valley. On a clear winter's day the Dead Sea can also be seen.

A short distance along Martin Buber Street a right turn leads to the **Brigham Young Mormon University**'s Jerusalem campus, which offers exceptionally fine views of the city. There are guided tours of the college on the hour. Carry on along Martin Buber into the Arab neighbourhood of E-Tur. Turn right at the end of Ruba El-Adawiya and follow the road round to the Seven Arches Hotel. From here, above the Mount of Olives cemetery, is the most glorious view of Jerusalem. There are usually several 'tourist' camels stationed here offering short rides.

Return along Ruba El-Adawiya and turn left down El-Mansuriya. Park where this steep hill meets Derekh Yerikho (Jericho Road) and visit the nearby churches, including the **Church and Garden of Gethsemane** where the gnarled olive trees certainly look old

*Garden of Gethsemane*

enough to have witnessed the betrayal of Christ. The church is Franciscan and has an impressive gilt mosaic above the entrance picturing Christ weeping over the fate of Jerusalem. Opposite is **St Mary's Church**, believed to contain the tomb of Mary, while up the lane to the right is the 19th-century Russian Orthodox church of **St Mary Magdalene** with its distinctive Slavic design incorporating seven gold onion-shaped domes.

*Israel Museum exhibit*

Drive up Derekh Yerikho and turn left into Sultan Suleiman. You are now skirting the Old City walls and the heart of Arab East Jerusalem. Turn left into Ha-Tsankhanim and continue on to Shlomo ha-Melekh (King Solomon Street) before making a right turn into Agron and proceeding straight via Ramban and Ruppin to the **Israel Museum** (Sunday to Thursday 10am–5pm, except Tuesday, 4–10pm, and Friday 10am–2pm and Saturday 10am–4pm) on the left at the junction with Kaplan. On your right is the Knesset, Israel's parliament. Stop for a coffee in the museum's cafeteria.

The **Dead Sea Scrolls** in the white-domed **Shrine of the Book** are the museum's most prized possession but it also has an absorbing collection of art, archaeology and Jewish ethnography tracing the foundations for the Judaeo-Christian heritage, plus an excellent children's wing. An initial browse can take several hours, but some visitors may want to spend much longer and also to visit the **Bible Lands Museum** opposite (Sunday to Thursday 9.30am–5.30pm, Friday 9.30am–2pm) which exhibits archaeological objects from the biblical Middle East. Several minutes' walk along Shderot ha-

*Shrine of the Book*

*Botanical Gardens*

Muzeonim is the **Science Museum** with imaginative hands-on exhibits for children (Monday, Wednesday and Thursday 10am–6pm, Tuesday 10am–8pm, Friday 10am–1pm and Saturday 10am–3pm).

The **Knesset**, opened in 1966, can also be visited (Monday to Wednesday during debates and Sunday and Thursday 8.30am–2.30pm for guided tours; admittance only on presentation of a passport). The centrepiece of the building is a 120-member chamber where parliamentary debates take place between the representatives who are elected every four years by proportional representation. The reception area contains a large tapestry of Jewish history designed by the artist Marc Chagall. Peculiarly, the Knesset chamber is downstairs from the entrance. This is because the original plan for the building called for the entrance to be located on the lower elevation of the southern side. But security officials pointed out, prior to the opening of the building, that Jordanian artillery in the West Bank several kilometres to the north could easily shell the entrance plaza. Opposite the existing entrance on the northern side is a Menora (candelabra), a gift from the British government.

Proceed down Wise and Burla streets, to the left of the Israel Museum. On your right are the **Botanical Gardens** (daily 8am until sunset). Tratoria Italiana, a kosher Italian restaurant by the lake on your right, is a pleasant location for lunch, or you may want to go to Bethlehem and eat in one of the Arab restaurants in Manger Square. To reach Bethlehem, travel down Ha-Rav Herzog, turn left into Ya'akov Pat and keep straight along Dov Yosef. At the traffic-lights at the top of the hill, turn left into Ha-Rosmarin and right down Highway 60 towards **Bethlehem**.

After travelling several hundred metres you will cross the border into the Palestinian autonomous zone. If there are any prevailing security problems, you will probably be prevented from entering. Otherwise continue on towards Bethlehem, which is now an Arab town. Almost immediately on your right is the **Tomb of Rachel**, the wife of Jacob. Take the left fork and continue on up to

*Church of the Nativity*

*Milk Grotto Street*

**Manger Square**. On your left is the Church of the Nativity.

The **Church of the Nativity** (open daily from dawn to dusk), is a large citadel-like building constructed in the 12th century by the Crusaders on the site of a Byzantine chapel, and today owned jointly by the Greek Orthodox, Catholic and Armenian churches. At the far end of the prayer hall are steps leading down to the **Grotto of the Nativity**. In the crypt, which is illuminated by candles, is a large star indicating the place where Christ is believed to have been born. Mary is said to have placed her newborn child next to the cave in what is today called the **Chapel of the Manger** and nursed him on the site of the **Milk Grotto**. The story goes that she dripped some milk on the floor in the process, hence the white colour.

It is a further 17km (11 miles) south along Highway 60 to Hebron. The **Cave of Machpelah**, where Abraham, Sarah, Isaac, Rebecca, Jacob and Leah are buried, is a fascinating shrine, but tensions between Jews and Arabs in the vicinity are such that it is not advisable to visit at present.

Drive back north from Bethlehem to Jerusalem along Highway 60. In the southern suburbs of Jerusalem turn right into Daniel Yanovski. After 500 metres on your left is the **East Talpiyot Promenade** and **Sherover Walkway**. This is a delightful park and recreation area on a sloping hillside commanding a superb view of Jerusalem and the Jordan Valley. There are several cafés which are ideal for afternoon or early evening tea.

Return to Derekh Khevron and drive towards Jerusalem. Turn left at David Remez and park by the railway station. This is a wonderful area to explore on foot. There are parks on both sides of David ha-Melekh Street and you can wander down by the windmill on your right and into the twee alleyways of **Yemin Moshe**, the first Jewish settlement built outside the Old City walls. At the bottom of the steps you stand before the **Valley of Gehenna**, leading down from the Old City walls through the **Sultan's Pool Amphitheatre**. It is worth booking tickets for a concert here: the atmosphere is incredible. Nearby, at the start of Derekh Khevron, is the **Cinemathèque**, where you can watch a golden-oldie movie, then eat on the balcony of the restaurant while enjoying the view over the valley to the Old City.

*Windmill at Yemin Moshe*

*Yad Vashem Holocaust Memorial*

## 3. Yad Vashem and Ein Kerem

**A morning reflecting on the barbarity of the Holocaust at the Yad Vashem Holocaust Memorial and Museum followed by a visit to the nearby village of Ein Kerem, birthplace of John the Baptist. Though a suburb of Jerusalem, Ein Kerem has a rural charm. After visiting the churches, you can travel to the nearby Hadassah Medical Centre with its beautiful Chagall windows.**

*–Though this tour is most conveniently accomplished by car, it is viable to travel by either bus or taxi (see page 33)–*

**Yad Vashem Holocaust Memorial and Museum** (Sunday to Thursday 9am–5pm and Friday 9am–2pm, no entrance fee) is located on the Hill of Remembrance overlooking the Jerusalem Forest to

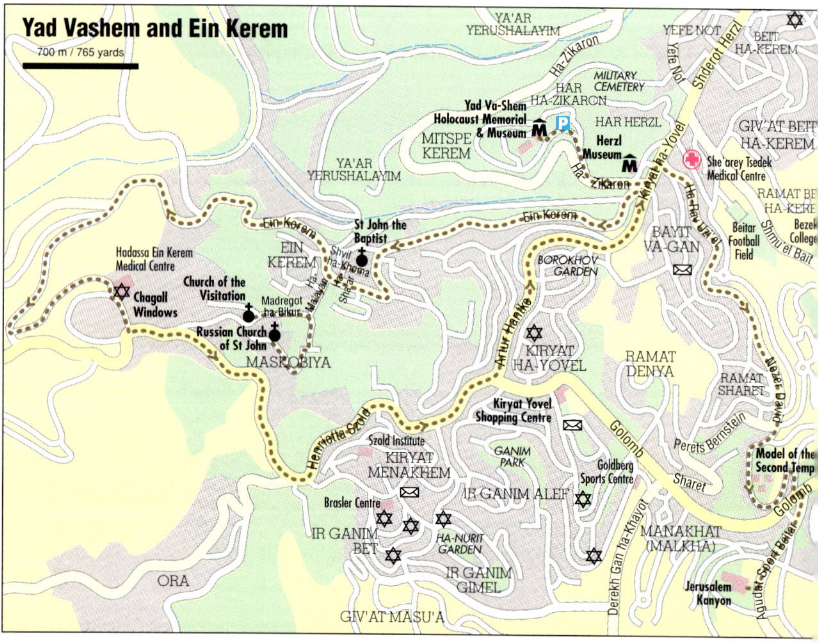

the west of the city. You can drive south down Shderot Herzl to the Mount Herzl Cemetery or take bus Nos 17,18, 21, 23 or 27 from the centre of town. Before Yad Vashem you may wish to get into an appropriately sombre mood by looking around the **Mount Herzl Cemetery**. This not only contains the graves of hundreds of soldiers who have fallen in Israel's wars but also the remains of many of the architects of the state, including Theodore Herzl, the founder of modern political Zionism. Perhaps the most striking grave, a simple black and white tombstone near the entrance, belongs to the former Prime Minister Yitzhak Rabin, who was assassinated in 1995 by a Jewish extremist, less than a year after being awarded the Nobel Peace Prize.

Coming out of the cemetery, turn right and take the first turning on the right which leads down to Yad Vashem. Walk towards the museum along the **Avenue of the Righteous Gentiles**. Each tree honours a Gentile who risked his or her life to save Jews. This provides a slim gleam of faith in humanity before the darkness and despair documented in detail by the museum.

*Holocaust Memorial Museum*

The museum uses enlarged black and white photographs, press cuttings and historical narratives to tell the grim story of the rise of Nazism, its anti-Semitic policies and the extermination of European Jewry during the course of World War II. This is followed by an exhibition of art by those who perished in the Holocaust, including simple crayon drawings by young children who died in the concentration camps.

Adjoining the museum is a small memorial chamber with the names, etched on black stone, of the concentration camps in which six million Jews and millions of other victims died. Back at the entrance, stairs up to the left lead to a memorial to the 1½ million Jewish children whose lives were snuffed out by the Nazis. This is symbolised evocatively by a dark corridor in which lights and mirrors represent the lives lost. Two to three hours is enough time to take in the harrowing details of the Holocaust, but those who wish to stay longer can stroll down to the **Valley of the Lost Communities**. Carved on the rocks are the names of the 5,000 Jewish communities from France to Russia that were destroyed by the Nazis.

There is no café at Yad Vashem and if you need refreshment you'll have to make do with an ice cream from one of the vans outside or back up the road at the cemetery.

After your visit, go back up Ha-Zikaron Street and turn right and right again into Ein Kerem Street by the round, red sculpture

*View over Ein Kerem*

which represents the sun setting. Before the precise time of sunset was published in daily newspapers, orthodox Jews and Muslims would come to this western point of the city so that they could perform their afternoon and evening prayers immediately before and after the sunset.

If you are travelling by bus, take the No 17 from the bus stop at the top of Ein Kerem Street. Travel down the road into the village of **Ein Kerem**, a fashionable suburb set in an attractive valley of terraced hills with olive trees and vineyards. Houses here are exorbitantly expensive and especially sought after by artists, who take inspiration from Ein Kerem's special charm.

Just before the central town square turn right into Ha-Sha'ar and then almost immediately right again into Shvil Ha-Khoma. On your left is the **Church of St John the Baptist** (weekdays 8am–noon and 2.30–5pm; Sunday 9am–noon and 2.30pm–4pm), built by the Franciscans in 1674 upon the ruins of a Byzantine chapel. It is believed that John the Baptist was born in the grotto which is now downstairs at the back of the church. Here bas-reliefs picture scenes from John's life and a Latin inscription reads: *Hic Praecursor Domini Natus Est* – 'Here the forerunner of the Lord (Christ) was born'.

Return to the corner of Ha-Sha'ar and Ein Kerem Street and relax over lunch at Le Chateau, a pleasing café-restaurant. After lunch, walk down Ha-Ma'ayan Street opposite the restaurant. As you turn right into Madregot Ha-Bikur (the Stairs of the Visitation), which leads up to the Church of the Visitation, you will see the spring

*The Church of the Visitation*

on the left from which the village derives its name – Ein Kerem is Hebrew for Spring of the Vineyard.

The **Church of the Visitation** (daily 9am–noon and 2.30–5pm, in summer 3.30–6pm) is also Franciscan. A modern, two-storey structure built in 1956, it stands on the site of the summer house of the parents of John the Baptist, Zachariah and Elizabeth. The name of the church refers to a visit which the Virgin Mary made to the couple's home. On the front wall of the church a colourful mosaic depicts Mary's visit to the site.

If you have some extra energy, visit the **Russian Church of St John** further up the slope. Go back down the steps and turn right into Ma'ale ha-Akhsanya. Turn right and right again to reach the church which also offers a splendid view of Ein Kerem.

The next leg of the journey to the nearby **Hadassah Ein Kerem Hospital** to see the Chagall windows cannot be done by bus, so if you do not have a car take a taxi from the town. Travel away from Jerusalem on Ein Kerem Street. About 1km (½ mile) down the road is a turning left to Hadassah. Follow the road round and leave your car in the car park just before you reach the hospital. Take the shuttle bus up to the hospital complex.

The **Chagall windows** (Sunday to Thursday 8am–3.45pm and Friday 8am–12.45pm) are in the hospital synagogue opposite the main entrance to the medical centre. The 12 richly coloured stained-glass windows represent each of the tribes of Israel. The location itself, however, is a disappointment, with the synagogue dwarfed by the large hospital buildings.

Drive back up Henrietta Szold Street to Jerusalem or take bus Nos 19 or 27. If you have time to spare you can detour to the **Model of the Second Temple** (Sunday to Thursday 8am–9pm, Friday and Saturday 8am–5pm). At the traffic-lights past the entrance to the Mount Herzl Cemetery, turn right into Ha-Rav Uziel Street and keep going straight for 2km (1¼ miles) before reaching the Model which is just past the Holyland Hotel. If you're travelling by bus, take No 27 from Hadassah and change to No 21 at Mount Herzl. The scale model shows how the Temple and Old City would have looked 2,000 years ago.

*Model of the Second Temple*

Beneath you is the **Jerusalem Kanyon** (shopping mall) with its stores, wide choice of cafés and restaurants and an eight-theatre cinema complex.

## 4. The Jerusalem Hills and Inland Plains

**Explore the countryside to the west of Jerusalem. Drive to the Sorek Cave, then on to the Beit Guvrin Caves. After lunch, return to Jerusalem via the Philistine archaeological excavations at Revadim.**

Drive out of Jerusalem on the Tel Aviv highway. After 7km (4 miles) at the end of a steep climb, take the exit marked Mevaseret and turn left. High in front of you is Kastel, the ruins of a Crusader fortress, which was the scene of bitter fighting during the Israeli War of Independence in 1948. If you fancy a climb, follow the orange signs and enjoy the view from the top. Afterwards continue southwards along the highway. After several kilometres there is a roundabout. Take a look at **Sataf** (straight ahead) where a biblical agricultural farm has been recreated.

Returning back up to the roundabout turn right and travel down Highway 395. After several kilometres, turn right onto Highway 386 and drive along the **Sorek Valley**. This is splendid countryside. The pastoral scene of hillside forests is sadly spoiled by the smell of sewage from the stream which runs beside the road, so keep your window closed. The railway, too, runs near the road. After 16km (10 miles) at the Bar Giyora Junction turn right onto Highway 3866. You are now driving along a ridge in **American Independence Forest** with attractive views on both sides. After about 6km (4 miles) turn right to the **Sorek Cave** (Sunday to Thursday 8am–4pm, Friday 8am–2pm).

*American Independence Forest*

Estimated to be 25 million years old, this cave was discovered in 1968 when the hill was dynamited for quarrying. Walkways and colourful lighting have been installed to display the stalagtites, stalagmites and other rare geological formations.

Return up the hill to Highway 3866 and turn right, continuing on to the junction with Route 38. Turn left and after the fast expanding town of **Beit Shemesh** you'll reach the attractive rolling green hills of the Valley of Ela where David is believed to have killed Goliath. This is wonderful hiking country; for an excellent view of the surrounding countryside and coastal plain turn right shortly after the junction with Highway 353 to the **Masua Observation Point**.

Carry on along Highway 38 to the junction with road No 35. Turn right and almost immediately on your left are the Crusader ruins of **Beit Guvrin**. But more remarkable are the caves to the left about

*Latrun Monastery*

1km (½ mile) off the highway. The National Parks Authority runs a series of tours of the caves, which originate from Roman times (Sunday to Thursday 8am–4pm, Friday 8am–2pm). None of these are natural caves. Most impressive are the **Bell Caves**, whose high, white concave roofs are the result of Roman quarrying. Nearby are underground burial chambers, and underground caves dug out for hideaway homes during the Roman period.

Returning to Highway 35, drive westwards towards Kiryat Gat. You are now driving along the northern border of the **Negev**, once a desert but today Israel's bread-basket. If you have time to spare for relaxation, travel straight on for some 5km (3 miles) to the **Khamei Yoav hot spring baths**, or just another 10km (6 miles) to **Ashkelon** with its golden Mediterranean beaches.

Otherwise, turn right at Kiryat Gat and travel north along Highway 40 to **Kiryat Malakhi**. If you are very hungry turn left at the junction with Highway 3 and almost immediately on your right is an Argentinian restaurant, El Rancho, which serves first-rate steaks. If you want a lighter lunch travel north along Highway 3, turning right towards Jerusalem at the Re'em Junction and then several kilometres afterwards turning right into Kibbutz Revadim. Have a snack at the kibbutz coffee house before proceeding to the remains of what was once the large Philistine city of **Ekron**.

Continue along Highway 3. After 22km (14 miles) is the **Monastery of Latrun**, a French Trappist monastery where the monks produce and sell wine, which goes well with the local cheeses sold in the small café behind the nearby Paz petrol garage. Pass under the Tel Aviv–Jerusalem highway and on the right is **Canada Park**, a recreation centre with vineyards, almond trees and playgrounds. Some believe that the ruins in the park are those of Emmaus, where Christ was seen after his resurrection (Luke: 24, 13).

Return along Highway 1 to Jerusalem, turning left after 10 km (6 miles) to Abu Ghosh. The café on your left at the Delek garage has a giant statue of Elvis Presley outside and is filled with Elvis memorabilia. Otherwise, turn left to Neve Ilan and enjoy afternoon tea in the guest house-café overlooking the coastal plain. You can hire horses from the stables if you fancy a trot through the forest.

Continue back up towards the Arab village of **Abu Ghosh**. There is an excellent roadside bakery opposite the junction to Kiryat Anavim

*Church at Abu Ghosh*

and good *hummus* at the restaurant opposite. Abu Ghosh itself has two Catholic churches (one with a large stone statue of the Virgin Mary) and a monastery, and is believed by many Christians to be the biblical Aminadav where the Ark rested after being rescued from the Philistines.

The road leads down to the Jerusalem highway. On the right by the highway is **Ein Khemed** (Aquabella), a landscaped, shady nature reserve with a broad stream flowing through it which is great for bathing on hot days. From here, it takes 15 minutes to travel back to Jerusalem – providing, of course, that the city's entrance isn't jammed with vehicles.

## 5. Wadi Kelt, Jericho and the Dead Sea

**A journey from Jerusalem to Jericho, one of civilisation's oldest settlements, located at the lowest point on earth near the Dead Sea. Have a dip in the Dead Sea, and visit Qumran where the Dead Sea Scrolls were found, and Masada, where Jewish zealots committed suicide rather than surrender to the Romans.**

*–Dress modestly for visiting the monastery; take your bathing costume. Sites closed on Saturday unless otherwise indicated–*

Travel north out of the city on Highway 60 (Derekh Ha-Shalom) to the Sha'ar Mizrakh interchange. Take the flyover which leads onto to Highway 1 on the right, and travel the 9km (5 miles) down to the Adumin Interchange then turn left towards Jericho.

After several kilometres you will find yourself in the heart of the Judean Desert. Barren, stark mountainsides billow off as far as the eye can see. Beneath you is the Dead Sea, the lowest point on earth at 400 metres (1,312ft) below sea level and part of the Syrian–African Rift Valley. Just after the junction with Highway 458, on your right, is the **Inn of the Good Samaritan** where Christ's encounter with the good Samaritan is said to have taken place.

*View of the Dead Sea*

After another 6km (4 miles) turn left to Mitspe Yerikho where an orange sign points to Wadi Kelt (Nakhal Prat). Turn left almost immediately before you reach the settlement of Mitspe Yerikho; the road heads briefly back towards Jerusalem before bending to the right.

You are now travelling on the ancient Roman highway linking Jerusalem to Jericho. After about 4km (2½miles) on your left is a signpost to **St George's Monastery** and a staircase down the side of the hillside into the mountain gorge. A small stream runs along the foot of the gorge leaving a ribbon of green through the desert. The Greek Orthodox Monastery nestles on the side of the hill surrounded by palm trees. Dating back to Byzantine times, the monastery has an ossiary containing the skulls of dozens of generations of monks.

*Detail in Hisham's Palace*

Climb back up to the road and continue down to **Jericho**. This route offers a marvellous view of Jericho, an oasis of green amid the desert. Before reaching the main highway, you will enter the Palestinian Autonomous Zone. You are now 270 metres (885ft) below sea level. Turn left at the main road and keep going straight until you reach the end of the road. Turn left and after another kilometre where the road swings to the right park your car: on your left is **Tel Jericho** (daily 8am–5pm). What makes the otherwise ordinary excavations here exceptional is that the walls are estimated to be 8,000 years old.

If you want to be spend longer in Jericho (which means you will not have enough time to go as far south as Masada in one day) other important sites include **Hisham's Palace** (daily 9am–4pm), an 8th-century winter palace with well-preserved mósaics. To get there, continue north along Highway 90 for 2km (1¼ miles) and then turn right. The palace is signposted.

Alternatively, a short way along the road leading west from the tel, there is a car park to your left and a path climbing up the mountainside to the **Monastery of the Temptation** (Quarantal). This Greek Orthodox Monastery commands a superb view of the Jordan Valley and Jericho. It is believed that Christ was brought here to be tempted by the devil. Back down at the corner of Highway 90, the Temptation Restaurant offers a good-value lunch.

*Flowers at Qumran*

Travel back south along Highway 90, turning left at the junction of the Jerusalem highway and right 4 km (2½ miles) to the east. Some 9 km (5½ miles) to the south, on your right, is **Qumran**. Visitors will be disappointed that the caves where an Arab shepherd found the Dead Sea Scrolls in 1947 can only be viewed from a distance. But they can learn about the Essenes, the ascetic Jewish contemporaries of Christ who possessed the Dead Sea Scrolls, and visit a reconstructed Essene settlement (Saturday and Monday to Thursday 8am–5pm). There is a pleasant restaurant on the site. Searches of the caves unearthed other scrolls and thousands of fragments, most of which are now on

*Mudbather at the Dead Sea*

display in Israel, either in the Shrine of the Book, at the Israel Museum in Jerusalem, or at the Rockefeller Museum in the formerly Jordanian part of the city.

The scrolls have revolutionised scholarship of the Second Temple period and thrown new light on the origins of Christianity, indicating that Jesus may have been an Essene, or at least was strongly influenced by the sect. The scrolls have revealed the mood of Messianic fatalism among the Jews of that time, explaining both the emergence of Christianity and the fervour of the Jewish rebels in their hopeless war against Rome. The scrolls have also disclosed much about the nature of the Essene way of life and the beliefs of the sect, as well as revealing details of temple ritual and worship.

Several kilometres further south is the **Ein Fashkah Nature Reserve** (October to March daily 8am–5pm, last entry at 4pm), an excellent place for taking a dip in the **Dead Sea**. The sea's high concentration of salt – about 30 percent – means you will float, but beware if you have any cuts as they will sting like hell. Despite the slimy sensation of the water, the Dead Sea is very healthy. Minerals such as bromine, iodine and magnesium act as sedatives to soothe the nerves, smooth the skin, and are especially beneficial for psoriasis, arthritis and rheumatism.

Hotels at **Ein Bokek** at the southern end of the Dead Sea offer treatment programmes supervised by medical professionals. Famous since the 1st century AD, the healing waters are believed to cure a spectrum of ailments, from skin disease to lumbago, arthritis and rheumatism. The clinics, run by doctors and nurses, offer sulphur baths, mineral baths, salt baths, mud baths, massage and exercise programmes; prices range from fairly reasonable to very expensive in five-star hotels, where the spas are actually on the premises.

Don't miss the mud if you do stay; Cleopatra is said to have sent slaves here to fetch it for her, and even today Dead Sea mud has

*Heroic Masada*

become a sought-after export as a natural moisturiser, earning some $600 million a year for the country.

After your float, rinse off in the showers or the nearby freshwater pools. Despite searing summer temperatures of 40°C (104°F) the risk of sunburn is reduced because evaporating gases from the sea form a mist that filters out many of the sun's harmful rays. The best time to visit the Dead Sea is in the winter when average temperatures here are about 21°C (70°F).

*Masada stone missiles*

Proceed southwards for nearly 50 km (30 miles) to the Misted Junction and turn right into the access road leading to **Masada** (daily sunrise–4pm), Israel's most spectacular archaeological site. Part of the line of cliffs which rise up to the Judean desert plateau, Masada is cut off from the surrounding area by steep wadis to the north, south and west.

It was on this desolate mesa that Herod the Great built an impregnable fortress as a retreat from his potentially rebellious subjects. Visitors to the site can wander through the magnificent three-tiered palace which extends down the northern cliff, the Roman bath house, with its ingenious heating system, the vast storehouses, the western palace with its fine mosaics and the huge water cisterns hewn in the rock. They can appreciate the remarkable desert landscape from the summit, which can be climbed easily from the west via the Roman ramp, ascended by cable-car from the east, or more energetically climbed via the 'Snake Path', also from the east.

These features alone make the fortress worth a visit, but it is the story of the epic siege of the fortress in the Jewish War against Rome which has made Masada a place of pilgrimage second only to Jerusalem's Western Wall.

In AD66, a group of Jewish rebels called the Sicarii (named after the *sica*, dagger, their favourite weapon) seized Masada from its Roman garrison, triggering the Jewish War against Rome. Securing their base there, the Sicarii proceeded to Jerusalem, where they took over the leadership of the revolt. In the bitter in-fighting between the rebel groups, their leader was killed and they returned to Masada to regroup. The new Sicarii leader, Elazar Ben-Yair, waited out the war at Masada, joined from time to time by other groups. He was still in possession after the fall of Jerusalem in AD70. In AD73, the Roman Tenth Legion arrived to put an end to this last Jewish stronghold.

With its auxiliaries and camp followers, the legion numbered over 15,000. Defending Masada were fewer than 1,000 Jewish men, women and children. Herod's store-rooms were well supplied. The Romans destroyed the aqueduct which fed the cisterns from dams in the wadi, but the cisterns held enough water for a long period and

*Metzoke Dragot overlook*

were accessible from the summit. The legion then constructed a wall around the rock, reinforced by camps, which blocked the main escape routes, and built an earth ramp, strengthened by wooden beams and shielded by stone, which pointed like a dagger at the perimeter wall of the fortress.

The final defences were set on fire, and when the blaze died down the Romans entered Masada to discover the bodies of the defenders laid out in rows. Repudiating defeat and refusing slavery, the men had first killed their own families and then themselves, drawing lots for a final 10 to carry out the act, one last electee killing the other nine and finally killing himself. This account in *The Jewish War* by Flavius Josephus has become one of the legends of modern Israel. In recognition of the symbolic importance of the site, young soldiers being inducted into the armoured corps today swear their oath of allegiance atop the fortress and vow: 'Masada shall not fall again'.

The excavations by Yigael Yadin in the 1960s uncovered the magnificence of Herod's fortress and palaces, but the most moving finds were of the Zealots' living quarters in the casement wall, their synagogue and ritual baths, the remains of the fire, and, in some cases, bits of their final meal. The skeletons of a man, woman and child were uncovered in the northern palace; more were found in a nearby cave, where they had apparently been thrown by the Romans.

On the summit, excavations of Herod's fortress-palace, including mosaics, are extensive and fascinating, but more eye-catching is the stunning panorama of the Dead Sea. From here, it's clearly apparent that the southern end of the sea is rapidly drying up and is already cut off from the northern body of the sea.

From Masada, return north to Jerusalem. Alternatively, if you want to stay overnight, there is a large cluster of hotels about 10km (6 miles) further south at Ein Bokek.

As you return to Jerusalem you may have time to do some hiking near **Ein Gedi**, site of a kibbutz and a nature reserve. There are two popular hikes – **Nahkal David** is the shorter (and usually far more crowded). After a 20-minute trek you will reach **David's Spring**, a cave covered by ferns beneath a waterfall. Tradition has it that David hid here from an angry King Saul. Ein Gedi is the home of a large variety of birds and animals, and if you're lucky you may see an ibex mountain goat, characterised by its long antlers.

Alternatively, you can hike up the attractive dry river bed of **Nakhal Arugot** to the south of Nakhal David. A 45-minute hike takes you to a waterfall, and there are pools higher up.

Return to Jerusalem the way you came, via Highway 90, but this time you should continue straight along Highway 1 at the junction to Jericho.

# Galilee

The Galilee is Israel's northernmost region. It is the greenest part of the country and its attractive mountain streams running down into the Sea of Galilee supply much of the nation's water. It is hard to believe that from here you are a two-hour drive from the desert.

This is also an area of profound religious significance for Jews and Christians. Christ lived in Nazareth and preached throughout the Galilee. Much of the Jewish Talmudic commentary on the Torah was compiled in Tiberias and the mystical Kabbalah texts were written in Safed. Sites such as the River Jordan, nothing more than a broad stream, and the tranquil Sea of Galilee, really an inland lake, offer idyllic rural serenity and sacred historical significance. Many pilgrims, disappointed by the religious 'Disneyland' of Jerusalem's Old City, find spiritual sustenance in the countryside of the north.

*Sea of Galilee at sunrise*

The Galilee reaches up to the troubled Lebanese border and sits in the shadow of Mount Hermon, whose highest Israeli-held peaks reach up to more than 3,000 metres (9,800ft). However, the Hermon and the Golan Heights to the south, a high ridge along the eastern side of the Sea of Galilee, were captured by Israel from Syria in 1967, and remain a bone of contention between the two nations.

Tiberias, built in AD20 to honour the Roman emperor of that name, is the region's largest resort town with a wide selection of luxury and budget hotels and youth hostels. It is a small, bustling town, 200 metres (650ft) below sea level with very hot summers but warm, pleasant winters. Visitors seeking a rural retreat can choose from half a dozen kibbutz guest houses and hundreds of bed and breakfast options in the Galilee's scattered settlements.

The two itineraries that follow both start from Tiberias.

## 6. Tiberias to Nazareth

**A morning's drive south to the Roman ruins at Beit She'an and westwards through the Jezreel Valley to see 20 layers of civilisations at Tel Megiddo. After lunch in Nazareth, focus on the Christian holy sites including the Church of the Annunciation and the Mount of the Beatitudes, Tabga and Capernaum on the northern shore of the Galilee.**

*– Most sites are closed on Saturdays –*

Drive south out of Tiberias on Highway 90. The hot springs around which the town was founded are on your left. In the following 11km (7 miles) a string of artificial beaches on the lakeside get unbearably crowded at weekends and holidays. One kilometre (½ mile) past the Kinneret Junction is the point where the River Jordan flows out of the Sea of Galilee. An orange sign points south to the **Yardenit Baptismal Site** where facilities are provided for pilgrims to undergo a ritual baptism. Yardenit adjoins Kibbutz Dganya, the country's very first kibbutz, founded in 1911 by Russian Jewish socialist pioneers.

*Baptism at Yardenit*

Travel south down Highway 90 through attractive countryside with steep mountain ridges to your right and the River Jordan snaking through the valley to your left marking the international border with Jordan. The newly opened border crossing with Jordan at Sheikh Hussein Bridge is only 7km (4 miles) from Beit

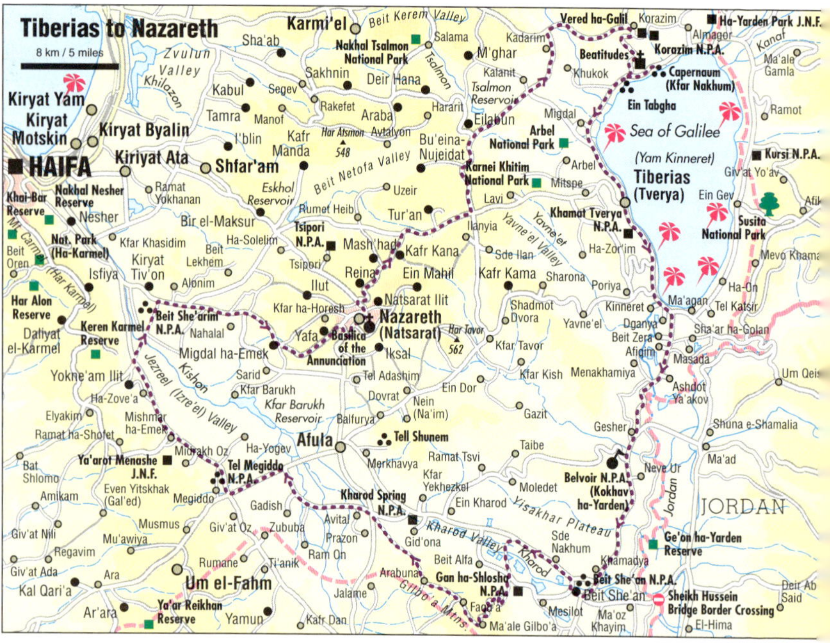

She'an, east along Highway 71. On reaching Beit She'an turn right at the first roundabout you come to and right again (the second turning has a Bank Leumi on the corner). The excavations are 400 metres/yards along on your left (summer, daily 8am–5pm; winter 8am–4pm).

*Roman capital at Beit She'an*

It is difficult to believe that **Beit She'an**, today a shabby town of apartment blocks, was once a member of the Decapolis, the 10 most important Roman cities in the Eastern Mediterranean, but the large amphitheatre which holds 6,000 people, the extensive baths and a colonnaded street go some way towards reconstructing its former glory.

From Beit She'an, travel west along Highway 71 towards Afula. This road passes through some of Israel's most beautiful countryside. If you have time to spare, travel into the **Gilboa Mountains** by turning left onto Highway 669, right onto 666 and right again along 667. You are now on the ridge of Mount Gilboa, which is especially delightful in the early spring when the Gilboa Iris, a rare, deep-brown flower, briefly blooms. There is also a splendid view of the Kharod Valley beneath you to your north. It was here that King Saul was killed in battle against the Philistines.

If driving along Highway 667, or the main Highway 71, turn left onto route 675 and drive through the equally luxuriant **Jezreel (Izre'el) Valley** where King Ahab was censored by the prophet Elijah for seizing a subject's vineyard. Turn left onto Highway 65 and right after 5km (3 miles) at the Megiddo Junction. A further 2 km (1¼ miles) on your left is **Tel Megiddo** (8am–5pm, Friday 8am–4pm).

*View of Nazareth*

Megiddo, one of the most fought-over sites in history, will, according to the Book of Revelations, be the site of Armageddon, history's final battle between good and evil. The archaeological site includes an explanatory museum but it can still be confusing, in part because there are remains from 20 layers of civilisation dating back to 4,000BC. The best preserved exhibits are a palace and the stables of King Solomon.

Proceed northwards along Highway 66 for 12km (7½ miles) and turn right onto Route 722 and right again 6km (4 miles) later onto Highway 75 which will lead you to **Nazareth**, Israel's largest all-Arab city and, of course, the home of Christ's parents. 'Can anything good come out of Nazareth?' asks John: 1,46. This rhetorical question might seem puzzling today, particularly to millions

*The Basilica of the Annunciation*

of Christians for whom Nazareth is equated with Christianity itself. But when it was posed two millennia ago, the feature that most distinguished this humble village in the Lower Galilee was its very obscurity.

Turn left off the main road into Paul VI Road and bear left at the first major intersection into Casa Nova to reach the Basilica of the Annunciation on your right. If you are keeping to schedule, and haven't been distracted by the Gilboa Mountains, it will be about 1.30pm and you may wish to grab a brisk, light lunch at the Astoria Restaurant which stands at the junction of Casa Nova and Paul VI roads.

The **Basilica of the Annunciation** (daily 8am–6pm), completed as recently as 1969, dominates the Nazareth skyline. Built of marble with no expense spared and with a large cone-shaped cupola, this is by far the largest church in the Middle East and is believed to be the spot where the Archangel Gabriel informed Mary that she had been chosen to bear the son of God. Elaborate murals in different national styles depict this story. Other important churches in Nazareth include **St Joseph's Church**, further up Casa Nova on the right. Built in 1914, the church is believed to be on the site of Joseph's carpentry shop.

Return to Highway 75 and turn left and left again at the major junction, leaving Nazareth northwards along Highway 75 and passing the new Jewish city of Natsarat Ilit. This route affords a splendid picture-postcard view of the city. Turn right along Highway 754 and right again at the Beit Rimon Junction after passing through **Kafr Kana**. This is one of Israel's two Circassian villages settled in the 1880s by Muslim tribesmen from Southern Russia who were warriors loyal to the Ottoman Turks.

After 6km (4 miles) turn left at the Golani Junction and travel north along Highway 65. Much of this highway offers an excellent view of the Sea of Galilee to the east. Turn right at the Nakhal Amud junction and right again 7km (4 miles) later at the Amiad Junction. Shortly afterwards, on your left, is the **Vered Ha-Galil Ranch**,

*Upper Galilee from the Mount of Beatitudes*

which you may feel warrants a return visit. Established by an Austrian prince, these extensive stables have horses to hire, an excellent restaurant and chalets to rent with superb views of the Sea of Galilee.

If you have kept to your schedule, the softer light and cooler breezes of the advancing afternoon will enhance your enjoyment of the Christian shrines on the northeastern shore of the Galilee. These churches have not been spoiled by the urban commercialism of Jerusalem, Nazareth and Bethlehem. Six kilometres (4 miles) after Vered Ha-Galil, also on your left, is the **Monastery of the Beatitudes** (daily 8am–5pm). Belonging to Italian Franciscan nuns, this octagonal church, built in the 1930s with neatly maintained gardens serenely overlooking the Sea of Galilee, is believed to be where Christ preached the Sermon on the Mount and chose his disciples.

Just down the highway turn left onto Route 87 and almost immediately on your right is **Ein Tabga**.

A Benedictine German monastery – the **Church of the Multiplication of the Fishes and Loaves** (daily 8.30am–5pm) – was built here in 1982 on the site of a 4th-century Byzantine chapel. It was here on the shore of the lake that Christ allegedly performed the miracle of the feeding of 5,000 hungry people with two fishes and five loaves. Adjacent to Ein Tabga is the **Church of the Primacy of St Peter** (daily 8am–5pm). Built in 1933 by the Franciscans in the distinct black basalt volcanic rock of the Golan Heights, this modest church marks the spot where Christ is believed to have appeared for the third time after his resurrection and where he ate with his disciples.

*Ancient Capernaum*

You'll have to hurry along to be in time to enter all these churches. Otherwise just enjoy the meditative quality of their pastoral and picturesque locations. Several kilometres further along to your east is **Capernaum**, believed to have been where Christ preached more sermons – including the Sermon on the Mount – and performed more miracles than anywhere else. The complex includes a museum, a Greek Orthodox monastery and a recently completed Franciscan church in the shape of a boat.

Capernaum was a metropolis of sorts in its heydey, and at least five of the disciples came from this Jewish town. It was after one of them, a simple fisherman called Peter, that the Galilee's most renowned delicacy gets its name. St Peter's Fish (*thilapia*) can be eaten for dinner along with French fries at the aptly named Restaurant of the Fishes and Loaves at Ein Tabgha or, more romantically, along the promenade at Tiberias after you've returned the 14km (9 miles) south along Highway 90. What St Peter's Fish lacks in flesh is usually made up for in good seasoning and presentation.

## 7. The Upper Galilee, Golan Heights and Mount Hermon

**A day's touring in Israel's far north. Travel from Tiberias up to Safed, known as 'Little Jerusalem', and then tour the Hula Reserve. Lunch at Metula on the Lebanese border and ascend the mighty Mount Hermon and the Golan Heights before returning to Tiberias.**

Travel north on Highway 90 along the borders of the lake for 9km (5 miles). After the junction with Highway 87 the road climbs into the Upper Galilee. Turn left after another 13km (8 miles) at the quaint village of Rosh Pina, one of the first modern Zionist settlements, established over a century ago by the Rothschilds. As you ascend, a superb view of the Hula Valley and snowcapped Mount Hermon lies behind you.

*Orthodox Jew in Safed*

After 10km (6 miles) you reach **Safed**, rather an ordinary town on first impressions. But the timeless charm of the town's enchanting alleyways quickly becomes apparent. Located more than 800 metres (2,642ft) high on a Galilee peak, a hilltop settlement has existed here since biblical times. In the 2nd century in Safed and the surrounding Meron hills local rabbis wrote the Kabbalah, the Jewish mystical texts, and in the 12th century the Crusaders built a fortress here. The town reached the height of its fame in the 16th century when hundreds of Jewish scholars flocked here after expulsion from Spain. The first printing press outside Europe was installed here in 1578 and the town became known as 'Little Jerusalem'. But in the 19th century Safed declined in importance after a devastating earthquake.

The narrow streets in the centre of town are jammed with traffic, so park your car near the bus station and walk up Jerusalem Street. On your right is the synagogue quarter and beyond is a far-reaching view of the surrounding hills. Take the steps down to your right – Ma'alot Olei Hagardom – and turn into the third alleyway to your right called Beit Yosef. Two lanes down on your left are several characteristic 16th-century synagogues; the entire neighbourhood is redolent of 16th-century Spain. If you want to stay longer in Safed, and have the energy to clamber up and down more steps, it is also worth visiting the Artists' Colony on the other side of the Ma'alot Olei Hagardom steps, and the Crusader fortress above Jerusalem Street.

Back in your car, return along Highway 89 to Rosh Pina and turn left northwards on Highway 90. On your left after 7km (4 miles) is **Tel Khatsor** where excavations have uncovered what was the most important town in Canaan as well as remains from Assyrian and Egyptian times. Many of the finds are on display opposite in the museum in Kibbutz Ayelet Ha-Shakhar (Sunday to Thursday

*Hula Nature Reserve*

8am–4pm, Friday 8am–1pm), but you won't have time to look around if you intend completing this itinerary in one day.

Another 7km (4 miles) north along the highway is a turn-off on the right to the **Hula Nature Reserve** (daily 8am–4pm). Until it was drained and used for agriculture in the 1950s the Hula Lake was a 4,000-hectare (9,800-acre) swamp-infested body of water. The reserve comprises the 80 hectares (200 acres) that was left to maintain the original eco-system including the world's most northerly papyrus thickets, a diverse range of birds and even water buffalo. All these can be seen from a raised wooden walkway. An additional 80 hectares (200 acres) of reclaimed farmland was recently re-flooded, and excessive peat residues which have plagued local farmers may compel the complete re-flooding of the valley, which will then become a tourist park.

Back on Highway 90, continue northwards. Pass through **Kiryat Shmona**, an unexceptional development town of 25,000 people, and carry on up the hill. As you ascend, the attractive **Hakhal Iyon Nature Reserve** with streams and waterfalls is on your right. You will soon reach **Metula**, an attractive settlement founded high in the hills in 1896 by the Rothschilds.

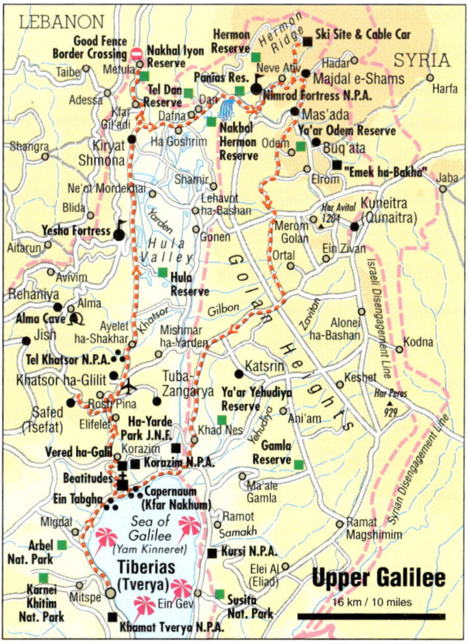


Standing in the main street of this serene holiday village it is difficult to realise that Metula's claim to fame is that it is surrounded by Lebanon on three sides. But a short walk through the apple orchards in any direction leads to barbed wire, which swiftly reminds you of the fact. Behind the main street is the Good Fence border

*Hakhal Iyon Nature Reserve*

crossing. Each day hundreds of workers from Southern Lebanon cross over here to work in factories in Israel. You can either have a quick snack lunch at one of the kiosks by the Good Fence, or if you have time enjoy a more leisurely meal at one of Metula's hotels or try some fresh trout at Kibbutz Dan (*see below*).

Go back down Highway 90 and just before Kiryat Shmona turn left onto Highway 99. In contrast to most of Israel this region is filled with small streams. These feed the River Jordan and supply about one-third of the country's water needs. At **Kibbutz Dan**, some 10km (6 miles) along the highway the Dag on the Dan restaurant will fish you out some of its fresh trout.

Six kilometres (4 miles) further along on your right is the **Banias Waterfall** (daily 8am–6pm), one of the main sources of the River Jordan. You are now officially on the **Golan Heights**, the land disputed between Israel and Syria.

Continue climbing Highway 99 and turn left onto Highway 989. Some 4km (2½ miles) along this road turn left to the **Nimrod Fortress** (daily 8am–5pm) overlooking the Hula Valley. Prior to 1967, this 13th-century Crusader castle was used by Syrian forces in attacks on Israel.

Carry on climbing up Highway 989 and turn left onto Highway 98. A further 8km (5 miles) and at nearly 2,000 metres (6,560ft), but still far from the summit of **Mount Hermon**, are a ski site and cable car. Depending on the amount of snowfall, these are open from about January to May. In the summer the site offers cooler temperatures, wonderful views and wild flowers.

Go back down the highway and stop for a coffee in the Druze village of **Majdal e-Shams**. The most conspicuous aspect of this sect, which broke from mainstream Islam in the 11th century, is that men are forbidden to cut their moustaches. Seven kilometres (4 miles) further south along Highway 99 is the **Ram Pool**, one of only two freshwater pools in the world formed in the crater of an extinct volcano.

Shortly afterwards you will pass through **Mas'ada**, another Druze village, and turn right onto Highway 978. The landscape is dominated by black volcanic rock which lends it a desolate air compared to the fertile valley below. At Ha-Shiryon Junction, turn right to Highway 91 and 8km (5 miles) down the road left onto Route 888 which runs parallel to the River Jordan, seen at its most attractive in the **Ha-Yarden Park**, just before the junction at Beit Tseida.

Return to Tiberias by turning right onto Highway 87 and, after skirting the northern shore of the Sea of Galilee, taking a left turn onto Highway 90.

# Haifa

Jerusalem prays, Tel Aviv plays and Haifa works. That well-known saying aptly describes Israel's third largest city, the centre of the nation's high-tech industries. But despite the port and the smoke-belching heavy industry to the north, Haifa is surprisingly beautiful, with resplendent Mediterranean panoramas from Mount Carmel, golden beaches and a rich cultural life. It is all the more surprising, therefore, that tourists tend to overlook the city. It makes a good base for exploring Akko (Acre) and the Western Galilee as well as the Mount Carmel countryside and the northern Mediterranean coast.

Haifa's origins are obscure, though it was probably established by the Phoenicians. Mentioned in 3rd-century Talmudic literature, the city was called Caife by the Crusaders but always remained in the shadow of Akko to the north. From the beginning of the 20th century Zionist settlers appreciated the potential of a deep-water port in Haifa Bay, although it was the British mandatory authorities who constructed the port in the 1920s. With an increase in maritime traffic and a steady stream of Jewish immigrants, the city's rapid development was assured. Today the Haifa Bay area has a population of nearly 500,000.

*Mediterranean view from Mount Carmel*

*Baha'i Shrine*

## 8. Haifa and the surrounding Region

**See the city from Mount Carmel and the Baha'i Shrine and Gardens and then drive north to Akko, Rosh Ha-Nikra on the Lebanese border, and the Montfort Crusader castle.**

*–This tour requires a car–*

Start the day with a view of Haifa Bay from **Central Carmel** (Merkaz Hacarmel) which is at the summit of the mountain and in the heart of the city's hotel district. Look down from the corner of Yefe Nof and Panorama streets. Fortunately the azure sea rather than the petrochemical installations to the north draw the eye and the industrial odours do not rise to the salubrious neighbourhoods on the peak of the mountain.

Return up Panorama Street and turn right into Shderot Ha-Nasi. At the end of the road down the hill, turn right into Shderot Ha-Tsiyonut. About 1km (1¼ miles) further down on your right is the entrance to the **Baha'i Shrine and Gardens** (daily 9am–5pm). The gold-domed **Shrine of the Bab**, completed in 1953, is the city's most conspicuous landmark. Containing the tomb of the Bab Mirza Ali Mohammed, who was executed in Persia in 1850 after proclaiming the coming of the 'Promised One', Baha'u'llah, founder of the Baha'i faith. The shrine stylishly combines the proportions of European architecture with Oriental designs; equally eye-catching are the surrounding **Persian Gardens** which it is claimed form the world's longest hillside garden.

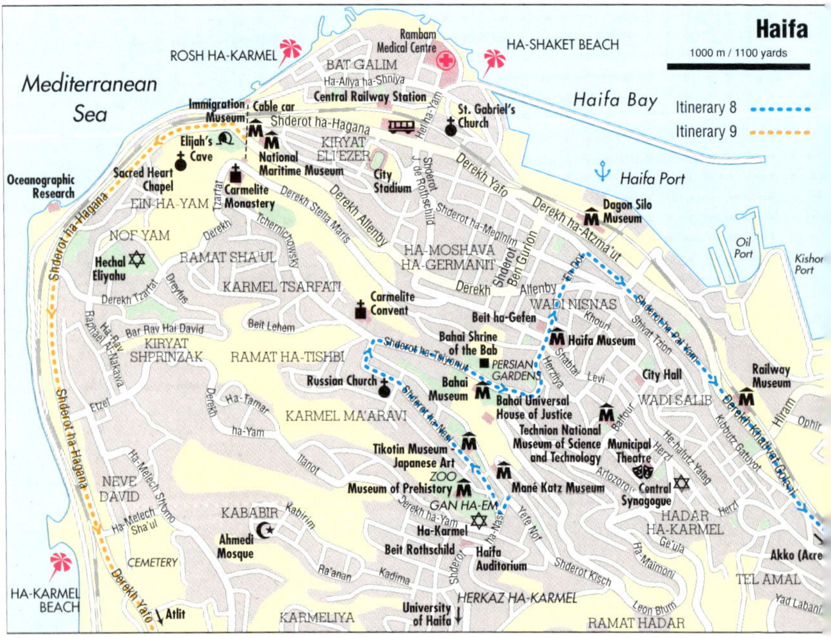

On the other side of Shderot Ha-Tsiyonut is the **Baha'is Universal House of Justice**. Closed to the public, this grandiose building, reminiscent of the Parthenon in Greece with 58 colonnades built of white marble, is the supreme council for the world's three million Baha'is, who live mainly in the US or under conditions of persecution in Iran.

*Akko street trader*

Leaving the Baha'i complex, continue down Shderot following its twists and turns, and go on into En Dor. At the end of the road turn right into Shderot Ha-Pal Yam and keep going straight along Derekh Hativat Golani, following signposts to Acre, until you reach Ha-Krayot (Checkpost) Junction. Turn left along Highway 4 and for 20km (12 miles) you will pass through a barren urban landscape of shopping centres, oil refineries and anonymous suburbs. This is the closest Israel gets to a landscape of heavy industry.

Eventually you will reach **Akko**. Turn left off the highway at the Ein Ha-Mifrats Junction and left again by the Palm Beach Hotel. Looking towards the coast you will already be able to see the Crusader sea wall and minarets of ancient Acre. Turn left again into Salah Ed-Din to reach the Old City. No other coastal city in Israel has as much history as Acre. The city was a seaport in Egyptian times, and under the Phoenicians it became an important trading centre, reportedly where glassmaking was invented. The Romans retained the city's name of Ptolemais, after the Egyptian Pharaoh Ptolemy who had captured the city in 261BC. The city reached its zenith during the Crusader period when it was renamed St Jean D'Acr. It was the last European stronghold in the Holy Land to fall to the Mamelukes in 1291. Acre remained a regional capital but went into decline after the British developed the port in Haifa in the 1920s.

*El Jazzar Mosque*

Park opposite **El Jazzar Mosque**, considered the most important mosque in Israel after Jerusalem's El Aqsa. The large green dome of El Jazzar, built in 1781, dominates the Akko skyline, though there is nothing exceptional to see within its confines. Opposite the mosque is the entrance to the subterranean Crusader city (Saturday to Thursday 9am–4.30pm, Friday 9am–12.30pm). This series of halls and courtyards – which was at street level nearly 1,000 years ago – was the quarter of the Knights Hospitallers. Tickets for the underground passages are also valid for the **Municipal Museum** (same opening hours) which can be reached by turning right at the exit and following El Jazzar Street around to the left. The museum, on your right, exhibits relics and drawings documenting the history of Akko. After visiting the museum, continue along El Jazzar Street to the Arab market. Although this is a relatively small bazaar, the few narrow alleyways have plenty of authentic oriental character. Afterwards, visit the fishing port. The fish restaurants around the marina make a pleasant place to enjoy lunch, and for a small payment you can go out to sea on a brief sightseeing trip. Return to your car along the sea wall, originally built by the Crusaders in the 12th century and reinforced by the Ottomans in 1799 after Napoleon's failed attempt to capture the city.

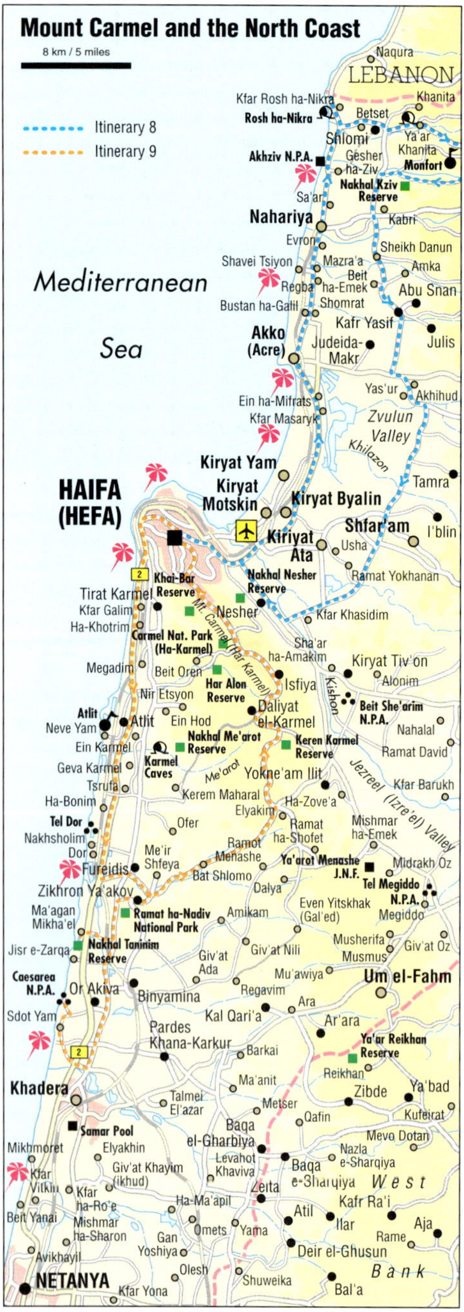


Leave the city via Weizman and Ben Ami streets and drive north along Highway 4. To your right several kilometres north of Akko is a well preserved aqueduct built by the Ottomans. Bypass **Nahariya**, a pleasant seaside resort popular with Israelis, and continue to Rosh Ha-Nikra, about 10km (6 miles) further north on the Lebanese border. The pick of the attractively deserted beaches around here is at **Akhziv**, several kilometres before Rosh Ha-Nikra.

The caves at **Rosh Ha-Nikra** are open from

*Elijah's Cave on Mount Carmel*

8.30am–6pm daily but close at 4pm on Fridays. They can be reached from the cliff-top by cable car. The unusual labyrinth of underground caves is partly submerged beneath water; visitors can stroll around the walkways with the relaxing sound of the waves swishing against the sides of these subterranean tunnels.

If you have made good time, cut inland along Highway 899 past the town of Shlomi and turn right after Kibbutz Eilon to **Montfort**, a French Crusader fortress (1266) several kilometres south on your right (Saturday to Thursday 8am–5pm and Friday 8am–4pm). The remains are less impressive than the hike through the Western Galilee hillside to see them.

On leaving Montfort turn right and right again to Highway 70 and then travel south towards Haifa, turning right onto Highway 75 and returning to Highway 4 just north of the Checkpost Junction.

Enjoy an evening in Haifa. Travel down the mountain on the Carmelit subway system, an underground cable car. The Hadar midtown shopping centre has a selection of restaurants and cheap *falafel* stalls at the corner of Ha-Nevi'im and Balfour *(see page 73 for suggestions)*. Down at the port there is a plethora of pubs and nightclubs as well as the city's red-light district.

## 9. Zikhron Ya'akov, Caesarea and the Carmel Mountains

**Drive south to the Rothschild's estate at Zikhron Ya'akov and then on to the former Roman capital of Caesarea. Return north via the Druze market village of Daliyat el-Karmel and Carmel Mountain National Park.**

*–Take a bathing costume if you might want to swim. Most sites are closed on Saturday.–*

Start your tour in Haifa with a visit to **Elijah's Cave** (Sunday to Thursday 8am–5pm, Friday 8am–1pm), on the southeastern side of the junction of Allenby and Ha-Hagana (Highway 4 running south out of Haifa). According to Jewish tradition, Elijah hid in this cave from King Ahab after killing the idolatrous priests. Christians believe that Christ, too, visited it with his parents, endowing the grotto with miraculous healing powers.

Drive south out of Haifa on Highway 2. Some 10km (6 miles) south of the city's southern entrance is Atlit. On the right off the highway are the ruins of a Crusader fortress built in 1200 and called the Castle of the Pilgrims. However, the site is not open to the public as it is within a military base and can only be viewed from a distance.

Another 11km (7 miles) south turn left at the Zikhron Ya'akov Interchange and travel along Highway 70. Cross the Fureidis Junction, where, to your left, is the Arab village of **Fureidis** and, on the hill to your right, **Zikhron Ya'akov**, founded in 1882 by Baron Edmond de Rothschild. Situated mid-way between Haifa and Tel Aviv, this is a prosperous middle-class town. Several kilometres further on turn right and drive through the town. Turn left onto Highway 652 and on your right is the entrance to **Ramat Ha'Nadiv** (Benefactors' Heights). Amid these beautifully designed gardens, with views of the Mediterranean, is the tomb of Baron Edmond and his wife Adelaide whose remains were brought here in 1954.

Turn northwards out of Ramat Ha'Nadiv and drive down the hill to the junction with Highway 4. Turn left and after 1km make a right turn where it is signposted to Ma'agan Mikhael. Cross the bridge over the motorway and follow the road round to the left. The **Nakhal Taninim** ('River Crocodile') reserve was, until the 19th century, the most northerly point inhabited by these reptiles in the world. The crocodiles are gone but if you are lucky you may see a colony of giant turtles. Otherwise just enjoy the river and its surrounding parklands. Cross the bridge over the river and stroll around the fish ponds, which during the spring and autumn attract hundreds of thousands of birds migrating between Europe and Africa. The beach on the far side of the fish ponds is usually delightfully deserted but you may prefer to go swimming in Caesarea.

*Ceasarea's Roman Amphitheatre and Crusader ruins*

*Roman aqueduct*

Back on the road, return to Highway 4 and drive southwards for about 6km (4 miles). Inland is the point where the Carmel mountain range ends and the flat coastal plain begins. After about 6km (4 miles) turn right to **Caesarea**, passing through the faceless suburb of Or Akiva and under the main Tel Aviv–Haifa Highway. The area has an air of affluence: on your left extends Israel's only golf course, while in the distance, to your right, is an exclusive residential neighbourhood.

The principal excavations at the **Roman Amphitheatre** and the **Crusader City** (daily 8am–6pm, Friday 8am–5pm), at what is considered one of Israel's finest archaeological sites, are where this road reaches the sea. Caesarea was built by the tyrannical Herod the Great in 22BC on the ruins of a Phoenician settlement. He constructed a sophisticated city, named after the Roman Emperor Augustus Caesar, which became the Roman regional capital after AD26 and was to retain this role for 500 years. At the time of Jesus, Pontius Pilate lived here, and St Paul was imprisoned here for two years before being sent to Rome from this port. The Crusaders, under Baldwin I, captured the city in 1101, and during the next 200 years Caesarea changed hands frequently enough to make a camel cross-eyed.

Most striking today is the beautifully preserved Roman Amphitheatre to the south of the Crusader City; it is still used for concerts. It was here that thousands of Jews were executed after their revolt in AD66. The Crusader City complex, contained within walls stretching for nearly 500 metres, includes houses, streets and churches from Crusader times as well as Byzantine remains; the original Roman jetty can be seen by the sea. Enjoy lunch in one of a number of cafés and restaurants around the car park opposite the site.

Afterwards, drive back east along the road and turn left to reach a picturesque beach which retains a major stretch of the original 17-km (11-mile) long Roman aqueduct.

*Galleries in Crusader City, Caesarea*

Drive back south past the Roman amphitheatre and Kibbutz Sdot Yam and get on the northbound side of the Tel Aviv–Haifa highway at the Caesarea interchange. Towering over you is the huge **Khadera Power Station**, a coal-fuelled installation which provides over 60 percent of the country's electricity.

Turn off the highway

*Right: Haifa from Mount Carmel*

*Musing Druze*

once again at the Zikhron Ya'akov interchange and head inland on Highway 70. After about 14km (9 miles) along this road, a natural valley cutting through the Carmel Mountains, turn left at the Elyakim Junction onto Highway 672. The road climbs 7km (4 miles) through pine forests to the hilltop Druze village of **Daliyat el-Karmel**.

Meander down the main street, which is the highway to Haifa, and look at the market stalls. Relax in a coffee house where the local Druze will serve you with their traditional friendliness and hospitality. Israel's Druze have been fiercely loyal to the state and are voluntarily conscripted into the army. They are proud of their economic and social success and integration into Israel.

Continue northwards along Highway 672 and through the Druze village of Isfiya. Afterwards you will enter the **Carmel National Park**, much of which was destroyed by fire in the early 1990s. The forest has grown back rapidly and the local wildlife includes deer and gazelles. You will re-enter the city on Mount Carmel near Haifa University. If you have time, take the elevator to the top of the high-rise building which dominates the campus and enjoy the view, which on a clear day extends to Mount Hermon in the north and Tel Aviv in the south.

One of the most pleasant places to have dinner in Haifa is at the Nof Restaurant in the Nof Hotel, 101 Shderot Ha-Nasi, near Central Carmel, where excellent Chinese cuisine combines with an amazing view of Haifa Bay lit up at night.

*Haifa at night*

Tel Aviv-Jaffa
600 m / 656 yards
Itinerary 10
Itinerary 11
Mediterranean Sea
"Reading" Power Station
Fire Brigade
Pedestrian Bridge
Diaspora Museum
Eretz Israel Museum
Planetarium
Tel Kasila
YARKON
PARK
Seminar ha-Kibutsim
KOKHAV HA-TSAFON
Sporteque
Bar Yehuda Bridge
The Naval Education Centre
TEL AVIV PORT
SHERATON BEACH
HILTON BEACH
INDEPENDENCE (HA-ATSMA'UT) GARDENS
Hilton Hotel
Tel Aviv Marina
GORDON BEACH
FRISCHMANN BEACH
TRUMPELDOR BEACH
Opera Tower
GE'ULA BEACH
Dolphinarium
Hasan Bek
CHARLES CLORE PARK
Etzel House
Beit Ha-Osef Museum
Clock Tower
Mahmoudia
Armenian Church
Andromeda's Rock
St. Peter's
St. Michael's Ch. (Greek Orthodox)
Israel Experience
JAFFA OLD CITY
Gesher Theatre
Flea Market
Museum of Antiquities
Noga Theatre
JAFFA CENTRE
GRONINGEN GARDEN
ZOOLOGICAL/ BOTANICAL GARDEN
HA-HAGANA GARDEN
Yad La-Banim
Beit ha-Khayal
Beit ha-Histadrut
Beit Liessin
Beit Lokhamei ha-Geta'ot
Bens Gurions' House
City Hall
Rabbinate
Court House
Museum of Art
DUBNOV GARDEN
Golda Centre
HA-KIRYA
Asia House & IBM Building
Camari Theatre
Dizengoff Centre
Rubinstein Pavilion
Mann Auditorium
Ha-Bima Theatre
Cinemateque
Z.O.A. House
History Museum
Beit Bialik
Betsal'el Market
Carmel Market (Ha-Karmel)
KEREM HA-TEIMANIM
Great Synagogue
Pagoda House
Ohel Shem
Shalom Tower
Ha-Hagana Museum
NEVE TSEDEK
Independence Hall
Suzan Dalal Centre
Aliya Market
NAVE SHA'ANAN
New Central Bus Station
FLORENTIN
SHAPIRA
Wholesale Market
MONTEFIORE
HA-RAKEVET
Central Railway Station
Diamond Exchange
BAVLI
GANEI YEHOSHU'A (HA-YARKON PARK)
Dekel Country Club
INDUSTRIAL ZONE
BITSARON
Cinerama
Beit ha-Shiryon
Municipal Sports Centre
Beit ha-Shoter
HA-TIKVA
Duhl Auditorium
Bnei Yehuda Stadium
Ayalon North
Ayalon South

# Tel Aviv

Amid the ancient, conservative urban centres of the Middle East, Tel Aviv is a brash young city which takes pleasure in ignoring tradition. Tel Aviv epitomises the re-shaped secular Jewish culture that the Zionist founding fathers wanted to take root. Tourists who have overdosed on holy sites and archaeology can lie back and enjoy the city's more hedonistic lifestyle, golden Mediterranean beaches and pulsating nightlife.

Established in 1909 as a garden suburb just north of the biblical port of Jaffa, Tel Aviv grew rapidly. Today it is the economic and cultural capital of Israel. Though the city itself has a population of only 350,000, it stands in the heart of a conurbation with more than 2 million residents.

## 10. Tel Aviv and Jaffa

**Discover the history of this region at the Eretz Israel Museum, mess about on the river and seafront, have lunch in Little Old Tel Aviv and enjoy the late afternoon and evening in Jaffa. This tour is done mainly on foot, though you may need to take a taxi or bus to the starting point.**

Start this tour at the **Eretz Israel Museum** (Sunday to Friday 9am–1pm, Saturday 10am–1pm), at 2 Levanon Street (formerly known as University Street). This is a one-hour brisk walk from the hotel district near the sea front or a bus ride (No 25) from Reiness (parallel to Dizengoff).

*Tel Aviv skyline at night*

The Eretz Israel Museum revolves around the excavations of Tel Kasila, an ancient settlement. Twelve layers of civilisation have been uncovered dating as far back as the 12th century BC. There are three Philistine temples from that period. Surrounding the tel is a series of pavilions with exhibitions of glass, copper, ceramics, coins and ancient tools found in the region, as well as a fascinating exhibit about the history of the alphabet and a Holy Land Landscapes Park which

*Boating in Yarkon Park*

vividly recreates the way farmers tilled the land in biblical times.

After leaving the museum on foot, cross Derekh Namir, and enter the **Yarkon Park** near the intersection with Shderot Rokakh. This is a tranquil, green oasis amid the hubbub and concrete of the city, though the nearby Reading Power Station belching smoke from its chimney will not allow you to forget the urban setting. If you are feeling energetic there are a number of places along the river which hire out rowing boats.

Leave the park by the Bar Yehuda Bridge and turn right immediately after crossing the bridge into Usishkin. Follow the road and the river round for several hundred metres before turning left into Yirmiyahu. Continue across Dizengoff and Ben Yehuda. You are now in **Little Old Tel Aviv** which was developed after 1936 when Tel Aviv port was opened at the nearby seafront – the Arabs who managed Jaffa port refused to allow Jewish boats to dock. Today the neighbourhood contains expensive apartments and fashionable restaurants and pubs. Try lunch at Mandy's Singing Bamboo at 317 Ha-Yarkon, as you turn left into Ha-Yarkon from Yirmiyahu. This fashionable Chinese restaurant was opened over 30 years ago by the British expat Mandy Rice-Davies, known for her involvement in the Profumo scandal which rocked the British government led by Harold Macmillan in 1963.

After lunch, stroll south down Ha-Yarkon and into **Independence Gardens** (Ha-Atsmaut). If it's hot and humid there should be a cooling breeze in this pleasant park on a cliff overlooking the Mediterranean (at night the gardens are a pick-up point for male homosexuals). Continue walking south behind the Hilton, the city's most prestigious hotel, and go down the steps to the Promenade (Ha-Tayelet) just before the Carlton Hotel, thus avoiding Kikar Atarim, a shabby square with restaurants and cafés. To your right is the **Tel Aviv Marina** which rents out diving equipment to qualified divers and offers courses for learners.

As you head south along the promenade you can either stick to the broad pavement, resting occasionally on the benches, or walk along the beach. The azure Mediterranean seems calm but a deceptively dangerous undercurrent drags some 100 victims each year out to sea and death by drowning.

On your left as you walk south, the city's hotels tower over the beach. Stop off at the **Opera Tower**, at the junction with Allenby, which contains upmarket souvenir and jewellery stores. In contrast to the salubrious surroundings of the Opera Tower, the first few blocks of Allenby Street consist of seedy, crumbling buildings and is the nearest Tel Aviv gets to a red-light district.

*Tel Aviv's family beach*

Continuing south on the promenade, it is better to keep your eyes out to sea. Much of the land near the coast is derelict, though new projects are gradually creeping south from the Opera Tower and north from the **Hassan Bek Mosque**. After the mosque, built by the Ottomans and recently renovated, is a complex of new hotels and high-rise office blocks.

Cross the highway and walk up Shenkar Street and straight on into Khevrat Shas. Turn left into Shabazi and right into Migdal. You are now in the heart of **Neve Tsedek**, which was founded as a Jewish suburb of Tel Aviv in 1886. Today, as the area is being gentrified, multi-million dollar properties stand beside ramshackle slums. The centrepiece of the neighbourhood is the **Suzan Dalal Centre**, on the right as you go down Migdal. This attractively renovated 19th-century high school is now a theatre and home to the Batsheva and Inbal Dance companies. There is a pleasant café here for afternoon tea.

Retrace your steps to the seafront and stroll southwards through Charles Clore Park and then along Goldman. You will soon find yourself approaching **Jaffa** (Yafo), the biblical port from which the Cedars of Lebanon were imported for the construction of the Temple, and from where Jonah set sail on his ill-fated voyage. Established 4,000 years ago Jaffa claims to be the world's oldest working port, though only fishing smacks and luxury yachts use the harbour today. Legend has it that Andromeda was rescued by Perseus from rocks close to the coast just as the sea monster was about to devour her.

After the Clock Tower (Kikar Ha-Sokhnut) take the next right into Mifrats Shlomo. Further down Yefet on the left is the **flea market**, although it is usually closed in the afternoon. Antique lovers may wish to return, for there are plenty of genuine bargains to be found on the stalls.

A few hundred metres along Mifrats look northwards to appreciate one of the best views of Tel Aviv. After the gardens there is a series of pleasantly quaint

*Jaffa minaret*

*Alleyway in Old Jaffa*

alleyways on your left containing expensive art galleries and souvenir shops. Old Jaffa oozes affluence and therefore lacks the character of equivalent ancient quarters in Acre and Jerusalem.

Though mentioned many times in the Old Testament, Jaffa has a Christian rather than Jewish feel about it. To the right of Mifrats Shlomo are several Greek Orthodox monasteries and churches, while at the top of the gardens is **St Peter's Franciscan Monastery**. Down the right-hand staircase called Shimon Ha-Burseki Street and on your left is **Simon the Tanner's House** (daily 8am–7pm) where (Simon) Peter is said to have received divine instruction to preach to non-Jews.

Continue down the stairs and enter **Jaffa Port** to your left. Around the port excellent fish restaurants offer a romantic setting for dinner. Try Taboon, which specialises in oven-cooked Mediterranean fish. If you want more modestly priced fare, go back up to Mifrats Shlomo. On the right, just before the junction with Yefet, there is a choice of a dozen fish restaurants which all offer good value for money.

## 11. The Diaspora Museum and Central Tel Aviv

**After spending the morning at the Diaspora Museum, the rest of the day is given over to getting to know Tel Aviv, including the Carmel Market and Yemenite Quarter, and Dizengoff. While you will need a car, bus or taxi to reach the Diaspora Museum, Central Tel Aviv is best explored on foot.**

The **Diaspora Museum** (Sunday to Thursday 10am–4pm, Wednesday 10am–6pm, Friday 9am–1pm) is in the Tel Aviv University complex in North Tel Aviv and can be reached by taking bus No

*Diaspora Museum replica*

25 from Reiness (parallel to Dizengoff) or by driving along Derekh Namir, turning right into Levanon and right into Klausner. The museum is mid-way along on your left.

When the museum was founded in 1979 it set a new trend, departing from the conventional idea that a museum should exhibit authentic objects. Instead this museum tells a story, the story of the Jewish Diaspora, using models, audio-visual material, etc. It encompasses almost every facet of Jewish heritage, culture, history and achievement.

After your visit, take the No 25 bus, or go by taxi or car back to **Kikar Yitzhak Rabin** at the junction of Ibn Gabirol and Bloch. This is the city's main square, previously known as Kikar Malkhei Yisrael. It was here, after a huge peace rally in November 1995, that Prime Minister Yitzhak Rabin was gunned down. A memorial stands at the foot of the staircase leading up to the City Hall on the north side of the square where the assassination took place.

On the southern side of the square, turn right into Frischmann and left into Kikar Masaryk. Walk down Ha-Melekh George, passing Dizengoff Centre, one of the city's main shopping centres, and continue on to the **Betsalel Market** in the streets on your right, just before the junction with Allenby. If you are under the impression that Tel Aviv is a European city, this market and the Carmel Market (Ha-Karmel) across Allenby will remind you that you are in the heart of the Middle East. It has a superb selection of fresh fruit and vegetables as well as pickles, dried fruits, nuts and cheap clothes. If you want an inexpensive lunch, stuff yourself with *falafel* (ground, fried chick peas in pitta bread) or *schwarma* (usually turkey in a pita) and as much salad and chips as you can eat, which cost very little at any of the many streetside kiosks.

If you want something more substantial, wander into the adjacent **Yemenite Quarter** (Kerem Ha-Teimanim). This crumbling old neighbourhood is renowned for its restaurants, and is the best place to sample the spicy, pungent Yemenite cuisine in authentic Arab-style stone houses. Try Zion in Pduyim, fourth on the right from the Carmel Market.

*Pumpkin for sale*

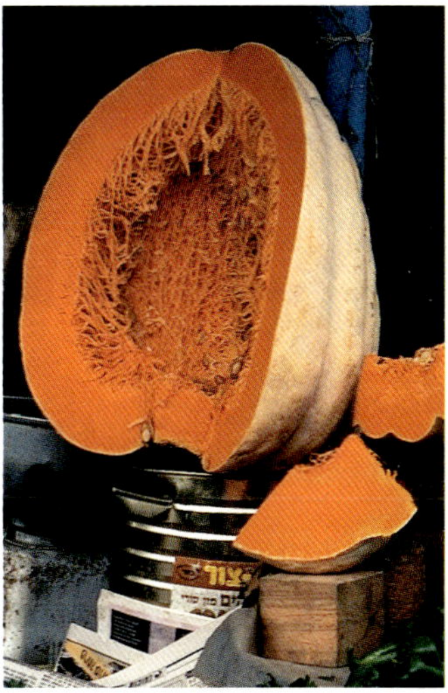

Midway through Carmel Market turn left into Shefer, and then left again at the end into the Nakhalat Binyamin pedestrian precinct filled with streetside cafés and buskers. There is a jewellery market here on Tuesday and Friday afternoons. Built in 1912 by and for artisans, the street has some interesting architecture.

Wind your way back across Allenby and bear right into **Sheinkin,** in the heart of the city's trendy bohemian district. Sheinkin has an eclectic mix of

*Habimah Theatre*

stores and cafés and there is even a religious section at the eastern end of the street. Six blocks along, turn left into Shderot Rothschild. Stroll northward up the central walkway of this shady boulevard, built in the 1930s by wealthy German–Jewish refugees. Its southern end is in the heart of the city's financial district and contains some of Tel Aviv's most attractive architecture.

Shderot Rothschild leads to **Habimah Square** (Kikar Ha-Bima). In front of you is the **Habimah Theatre**, Israel's national theatre company originally founded in Russia early in the 20th century. On the far right corner of the cultural complex is the **Mann Auditorium**, home of the Israel Philharmonic Orchestra. Turn left out of Rothschild and immediately right into Tarsat. On the corner with Dizengoff is the **Helena Rubinstein Pavilion** (Sunday to Thursday 10am–9.30pm, Friday 10am–2pm, Saturday 7–10pm) exhibiting contemporary Israeli and overseas art.

If this whets your appetite for more art, walk over to the **Tel Aviv Museum of Art** (same opening hours), the largest museum in Israel devoted to the fine arts. Its comprehensive collection includes paintings by Picasso, Renoir, Monet, Van Gogh and the like. The museum is reached by crossing over into Shderot Khen and turning right into Ha-Nevi'im and over into Shderot Shaul Ha-Melekh. Enter left just past the new Tel Aviv Centre for the Performing Arts (home to the Israel Opera, Carmeri Theatre Company and Rishon Le Zion Symphony Orchestra).

Otherwise, turn left outside the Helena Rubinstein Pavilion and stroll down **Dizengoff**. Named after the first mayor of the city, this was once Tel Aviv's grandest avenue and **Dizengoff Circle** (Kikar Dizengoff) was considered the heart of the city. Dizengoff, once regarded as a cross between the Via Veneto and Fifth Avenue, is no longer the place to see and be seen, but it remains popular with young and old alike out for an evening stroll. Turn left at Gordon into the heart of the city's art gallery district. Don't be bashful about entering galleries just to look around.

*Outside the Dizengoff Theatre*

If you want to finish the evening with a good steak supper, try White Hall in Mendele, reached by turning left into Ben Yehuda and heading back south for a block and a half before turning right. If you prefer fish, try Pundag in nearby Frishmann.

# Eilat

Nestling attractively beneath desert mountains on the northern tip of the Red Sea, Eilat is Israel's southernmost city. Its abundant winter sunshine, with average January temperatures of 21°C (70°F), and its colourful marine life are a great draw to tourists (though this area is best avoided from May to September when daytime temperatures usually climb above 40°C (104°F) .

King Solomon set up a flourishing port city here to the east of Eilat – known as Etzion Geber in biblical times – where Jordan's Aqaba is today. The Israeli army established a Red Sea outlet for modern Israel during the War of Independence, and Eilat was officially founded in 1950. In recent years Eilat has rapidly emerged as the country's most popular tourist destination after Jerusalem. Its port has expanded along with trade to Japan, South Korea and the Far East.

*Mitspe Ramon Visitors' Centre*

Eilat sits in the Syrian–African rift valley at the point where the Negev Desert stretching down from the Jordan Valley and the Dead Sea meets the Red Sea. The surrounding mountains to east and west turn delightful shades of pink, red and orange depending on the time of day.

The town makes an ideal base for exploring both the Sinai Desert in Egypt via the Taba border crossing 9km (5 miles) south of the city, and Jordan, which can be accessed from the Eilot frontier point just north of the city.

## 12. Eilat, the Negev, and the Red Sea

**After some early-morning birdwatching, drive north to the Hai–Bar Nature Reserve to see the region's wildlife. Return via King Soloman's Pillars, then take an afternoon trip to Dolphin Reef and the Coral World Underwater Observatory.**

Bird-lovers may wish to start their day very early at the observation point, ringing station and hiking trails to the northeast of the hotel district. Eilat is an ornithologist's paradise as millions

*Spotting the birdlife*

of birds migrating between Europe and Africa along the rift valley alight here each spring and autumn. Regular feathered visitors include 30 different species of raptors, among them five different types of eagle, as well as an impressive 400 kinds of songbirds, water fowl and seabirds. Details of early morning activities are available from the **International Birdwatching Centre** (daily from dawn–9.30am) at 61 Mercaz Tzenter (opposite the bus station), tel: 07-6374276. The observation centre can be reached either on foot or by car from a track off to the left of the road running north of the lagoon – simply follow the signposts.

You may wish to see some larger animals at the **Hai-Bar Nature Reserve** in the Arava Valley. This can be reached by driving north along Highway 90 for some 40km (25 miles) to Kibbutz Yotvata (this kibbutz has a reputation for producing the best milk products in Israel, so try some fresh milk at the cafeteria by the filling station). Tours of Hai-Bar leave daily at 9am, 10.30am, noon and 1.30pm. Before taking the 90-minute tour, visit the **Arava Visitors' Centre** (included in the price of the ticket) which exhibits information about the geological history, flora and fauna of the region. It is preferable to take the earliest tour (this may not be possible if you have already gone birdwatching), because the animals tend to go to sleep as the day warms up.

The reserve, extending over 8km (5 miles) to the south of Yotvata and covering 3,240 hectares (8,000 acres) features animals which historically lived in the region and have been successfully reintroduced, including wild asses, gazelles and ostriches. Some have already been released into the wild. There is a predators' compound in the centre of the reserve in which deadly snakes and other reptiles and wild cats, including leopards, are kept in zoo conditions.

If you want to explore the desert further and you are in Eilat for several days, you may wish to travel the 90km (56 miles) or so north to **Mitspe Ramon**. This giant crater, measuring 40km (25 miles) by 8km (5 miles) and formed 200 million years ago, has layers upon layers of exposed coloured rock enabling geologists to understand how the crater evolved. The crater can be reached by travelling north along Highway 90 and turning left onto Highway 40 10km (6 miles) after Yotvata at the Ktura Junction. Start off at the Visitors' Centre above the crater (daily 9am–4.30pm, Friday 9am–2pm) which explains this rare geological phenomenon and offers a splendid view of the crater.

Otherwise, return south and visit **Timna Park** by turning left at Bikat Timna Junction just after Elifaz 13km (8 miles) south of Yotvata. The road winds through an attractive canyon and after 8km (5 miles) reaches **King Solomon's Pillars**, a natural and impressive rock formation caused by erosion. This area is filled with copper mines – the famous King's Solomon's Mines – exploited for over 4,000 years until closed on economic grounds in the 1970s.

Points of interest on the highway south to Eilat are the world's most northerly Dom Palm tree (signposted several hundred metres east of the highway about 10km/6 miles north of Eilat) and the border crossing to Jordan, reached along Highway 109 running east from the Eilot Junction 3km (2 miles) north of Eilat.

*Coral World Underwater Observatory*

Return to Eilat for lunch. Try the Blue Fish restaurant for reasonable value seafood on the seafront by the Moriah Hotel. Then drive south towards the Egyptian border. Just after the port is the **Dolphin Reef** (daily 9am–5pm), a private beach where you can swim and meet the dolphins. You can even hire diving equipment (if you have a licence) and dive with the dolphins, or with a qualified instructor. The dolphins are extremely friendly and are used in therapeutic programmes for disabled children. Several years ago a group of British women attempted to give birth but the local health authorities intervened to stop them.

Several kilometres further south is the **Coral Beach**, a quieter alternative to the main beach in town. To the west of Coral Beach is the entrance to the Red Canyon, where eager hikers can climb the 700 metres (2,300ft) up Mount Yehoshafat to enjoy a splendid aerial view of Eilat and the Red Sea. At the southern tip of Coral Beach is the highly recommended **Coral World Underwater Observatory** (8.30am–5pm, Friday 8.30am–3pm). Through its underwater windows are delightful and unbelievable fish of all shapes, sizes and colours as well as peculiar coral and rock formations. There is also an attractive aquarium with selected fish and a pool containing sharks and rays, and you can hire glass-bottom boats to go out to sea or submerge yourself in the yellow submarine.

Above the observatory is an attractive circular-shaped café where you can order afternoon tea.

Several kilometres further south is the Taba border crossing to Egypt. If you are staying in Eilat for a week or so, try taking an organised tour to the Sinai Desert peninsula, a rugged, spectacular desert with Red Sea beaches and sites of religious significance such as **St Catherine's Monastery** on Mount Sinai where it is believed Moses received the Ten Commandments.

*St Catherine's Monastery*

# Shopping

When it comes to shopping, Israel is where East truly meets West. You can either browse through department stores in the air-conditioned comfort of shopping malls or haggle in traditional markets. But, apart from the ethnic experience of oriental markets, and the need to take home souvenirs and gifts, or maybe items of religious significance, there is very little reason to shop in Israel. Because the cost of living is high, you can expect to pay anything from 10 to 50 percent more than the equivalent for consumer goods in Western Europe and more than double the North American price.

## Shopping Hours

Stores usually open 9am–7pm Sunday to Thursday, and 9am–1pm on Friday. Shops are closed on Saturday but often open after dark until midnight. Some suburban stores may take a siesta from 2–4pm, and Arab markets are open all day Friday and Saturday.

## Markets

The souk is at the heart of Arab culture and strolling around the market in Jerusalem's Old City's Muslim Quarter is a must for a taste of the Orient. Enter the market either by Jaffa Gate or Damascus Gate and enjoy the chaotic hubbub, the smell of spices and the good-natured banter of the shopkeepers. This is not the place to shop if you are embarrassed by haggling, and you can buy all the same items in West Jerusalem at fixed prices (try the Ben Yehuda Street mall) and possibly pay less. Nevertheless, it is still worth coming to the Arab market to sit in a café and sip coffee, eat *bahlawe* and perhaps smoke a *narghile* (water pipe).

*Experience the Souk*

If you want to buy in the souk, then the professional way to do it is to price objects in the stores of West Jerusalem first. This will accurately indicate what you should be paying and help you haggle with confidence. Items of interest in the souk include olive wood carvings, *kaffiyehs* (Arab headscarves), which are popular in the west as a fashion accessory, Hebron glassware, copper and brassware including coffee

*Sophisticated shopping mall*

trays, ceramics (especially attractive are Armenian tiles), basketware, and T-shirts, emblazoned with a range of Hebrew, Arabic and English slogans.

Similar souvenirs and other goods can also be bought cheaply in Akko, Nazareth and Bethlehem. Other markets worth visiting are in the Druze village of **Daliyat el-Karmel** (but prices are more expensive here because this market tends to be fashionable with Israelis); the Thursday morning Bedouin market in **Be'er Sheva**, which is a marvellous experience, not so much for your own bargains as to see local people bartering over the value of a camel or goat; and the flea market in **Jaffa**, which is good for antiques.

The **Mahane Yehuda Market** in Jerusalem and the **Karmel Market** in Tel Aviv are excellent food markets.

## Shopping Malls

There is nothing very Middle Eastern about these places but they can be the most comfortable and convenient places to buy gifts, especially if you are travelling with children. Try the **Malkah Mall** in Jerusalem or the **Dizengoff Centre** in Tel Aviv. Malls also have a wide range of fast food outlets and multi-theatre cinemas.

## Antiquities

If you want to go home with a piece of the region's archaeological heritage, then Israel is the only country in the Middle East in which it is legal to buy antiquities – providing the vendor can supply a certificate from the government's Department of Antiquities. Stores in Jerusalem's **House of Quality** (Derech Khevron near the Cinematheque) such as Guy Gallery (Tel: 02-6725111), or in **Khutzot Hayotzer** opposite the Jaffa Gate, or in Jaffa's gallery quarter, specialise in such items as shekel coins dating from biblical times and ancient oil lamps, which can be purchased for very modest sums.

*Antique coins on sale*

For Judaica try **Sam Philipe**, 18 King David Street (David Ha-Melekh), Jerusalem, tel: 02-6259928, or **Tel Aviv Ramada Hotel**, Ha-Yarkon Street, Tel Aviv, tel: 03-5226897.

## Diamonds and Jewellery

Israel is the world's largest supplier of polished diamonds and the valuable stones can be purchased for 20 percent less than in Europe. The best diamond stores are either near the Diamond Exchange in Ramat Gan, outside Tel Aviv, or in Netanya, which has

*Impulse buys*

a large diamond cutting and polishing industry.

The **National Diamond Centre** is one of the country's largest chains. Main branches at:
143 Bethlehem Road, Jerusalem, tel: 02-6733770; 90 Herzl Street, Netanya, tel: 09-8624770; 17 Abba Hillel Street, Ramat Gan, tel: 03-7518930.

A lot of reasonably priced hand-made jewellery is on sale in Jerusalem's **Ben Yehuda Street Mall** and outside Beit Agron at the end of Salomon Street, Jerusalem. It is also found in Tel Aviv's **Nahalat Binyamin Street** on Tuesdays and Fridays.

## Leather Goods

Though still expensive, leather can be 35 percent cheaper than in Europe. **Beged Or** runs a chain of leather stores around the country including one at 2 Ben Yehuda Street, Jerusalem, and another in Tel Aviv's Dizengoff Centre.

## Newspapers, Books, Maps, etc.

These items, including the latest journals from Europe and North America, can be acquired from countless stores. The best selection of English-language newspapers and books is offered by **Steimatsky** with branches in Jerusalem and Tel Aviv:
Steimatsky, 39 Yaffo Street, Jerusalem, tel: 02-6250155; and at 109 Dizengoff Street, Tel Aviv, tel: 03-5221513.

## Duty Free and VAT

There are duty-free stores at Ben Gurion and Eilat airports as well as in tourist districts (goods purchased are delivered direct to the airport). The **James Richardson** duty-free shop at Ben Gurion Airport sells many of the world's best known brands of spirits and cigarettes more cheaply than in European airports.

Shops displaying a sign 'Recommended by the Ministry of Tourism' will offer a 5 percent discount on purchases of more than $50.

VAT of 17 percent is refundable provided the invoice amounts to more than $50 (about £35) and is sealed inside a transparent bag with the goods, so that both the goods and the invoice can be seen when presented to the bank in the departure hall at the airport. Refunds are made in dollars. This does not apply to tobacco, electrical products or photographic equipment.

## Complaints

If you feel you have been cheated – not simply that you have paid too high a price, but given faulty goods that a store refuses to change – then contact the Ministry of Industry and Trade's Consumer Division, tel: 03-5604671.

# Eating Out

Israeli cuisine reflects the cosmopolitan make-up of the population and also the fashionable preferences of the West. In addition to traditional Middle Eastern cooking there are plenty of Chinese, Italian, French and Indian restaurants to choose from, as well as the usual range of fast food outlets offering hamburgers, French fries, pizzas and sandwiches. Fish and meat are often disappointing. Local fish are leaner than the varieties caught in Europe and America, and meat, which according to kosher laws must have all its blood drained out, is often desiccated.

Kosher law requirements also mean that meat and dairy products cannot be served together, so don't expect butter on your bread when eating meat, or milk in your coffee afterwards. This distinction is significant for vegetarians, who can be assured of meat-free meals in dairy restaurants. However, many restaurants, especially in Tel Aviv and Eilat, are not kosher. Visitors may be disappointed to find that traditional Ashkenazi Eastern European cooking is very difficult to find.

Israelis enjoy their food and generally restaurants serve large portions. Hotels often try too hard to accommodate English-speaking guests and as a result make their food too bland. Generally hotels serve a large buffet breakfast with lots of fruit, vegetables, fish, cheeses and cereals, so that lunch need only be a snack. Most recommended in this department are the delicious and inexpensive Middle Eastern hors d'ouevre salads such as *hummus*, *tehina* (sesame seeds), *taboule*, etc, all eaten with pitta bread.

Service, even in very expensive Israeli restaurants, tends to be informal and sloppy. Partly because of this, expensive Israeli restaurants can be disappointing when compared with similar establishments in Europe. On the other hand, the average standard of cuisine in Israel is high and if you take pot luck and stop at an ordinary looking roadside restaurant you're likely to be pleasantly surprised.

Very cheap and very healthy are the *falafel* bars, usually near central bus stations, where you get spicy fried chick-pea balls in pitta bread with chips and as much salad as you can eat.

In the following guide, price categories per person, excluding drinks, are: $ – inexpensive; $$ – moderate; $$$ – expensive.

***Mezze platter***

## Jerusalem

**MISHKENOT SHA'ANANIM**
*Yemin Moshe (behind the windmill)*
*Tel: 02-6254424*
High quality French cuisine (not kosher) with an inspirational view of the Old City. Try the filet steak. $$$

**COW ON THE ROOF**
*Jerusalem Sheraton Plaza Hotel*
*King George Street*
*(Ha-Melekh George)*
*Tel: 02-6228133*
One of the city's oldest restaurants. Excellent beef dishes as the name implies, but it is in the hotel's basement rather than on the roof. Kosher. $$$

**TANDOORI**
*Holiday Inn Crowne Plaza*
*Givat Ram*
*Tel: 02-6588867*
One of a chain of kosher Indian restaurants (don't expect yogurt on your tandoori) with an excellent selection of vegetarian dishes. $$

**PHILADELPHIA**
*9 Alzaharra Street*
*East Jerusalem*
*Tel: 02-6289770*
This is Jerusalem's best known and most popular Arab-owned restaurant. Best of all is the wide selection of hors d'oeuvre. Not kosher. $$

**THE YEMENITE STEP**
*10 Yoel Salomon Street*
*Tel: 02-6240477*
Selection of traditional Yemenite foods. Try the *malahwah* pancakes. $

**NORMAN'S BAR & GRILL**
*27 Emek Refaim Street*
*German Colony*
*Tel: 02-5666603*
For lovers of thick, juicy American-style hamburger steaks. It's kosher, so don't expect cheeseburgers. Does a very good business lunch. Has a large garden and is located in the trendy German colony. $

**EUCALYPTUS**
*7 Horkanos Street*
*Tel: 02-6244331*
Billed as a restaurant offering the ancient recipes of the Land of Israel, the owner/chef clearly has a way with herbs and spices. Try the sorrel soup and generally trust his recommendations. Kosher. $

## Tel Aviv

**ZION**
*28 Pduyim Street*
*Kerem Ha-Teimanim*
*Tel: 03-5178714*
The pick of the restaurants in Tel Aviv's ethnic Yemenite quarter. The exclusive section offers choicer cuts of

***Philadelphia Restaurant***

meat than the 'regular', more modestly priced restaurant downstairs. Kosher. $$$

**Takamaru**
*4 Ha'Arba'a Street*
*Tel: 03-5621629*
One of only a few Japanese restaurants in Israel. Not kosher. Will not disappoint fans of Japanese food. $$$

**Taboon**
*Jaffa Port*
*Tel: 03-6811176*
Excellent fish restaurant romantically located by the quayside where Jonah set sail for Nineveh. Speciality of the house is oven-baked fish. $$

**White Hall**
*6 Mendele Street*
*Tel: 03-5249282*
Great steaks and good choice of salads to go with them. $$

**Mandy's Singing Bamboo**
*317 Ha-Yarkon Street*
*Little Old Tel Aviv*
*Tel: 03-6051282*
The city's best-known Chinese restaurant in trendy uptown neighbourhood. $$

**Alexander Café Restaurant**
*76 Herbert Samuel Street*
*Tel: 03-5105585*
A good choice of Middle Eastern, French and Italian dishes. View of the sea. $

## Haifa and the North

**Nof Chinese Restaurant**
*Nof Hotel*
*101 Ha-Nasi Boulevard*
*Haifa*
*Tel: 04-8354311*
Enjoys a splendid view of Haifa Bay and the Mediterranean. $$$

***Fresh-caught fish***

**The House (Habayit)**
*Opposite Lido Beach*
*Tiberias*
*Tel: 06-6792353*
Chinese cuisine. Considered one of the best restaurants in Israel. $$$

**Dolphin Sea Food Restaurant**
*13 Bat Galim Avenue*
*Haifa*
*Tel: 04-8523837*
A wide selection of well seasoned charcoal-grilled fish. Located near the sea front. $$

**Moshav Amirim**
*Merom Ha-Galil*
*Tel: 06-6987365*
This vegetarian village has several restaurants catering imaginatively for the vegetarian palate. $$

## Eilat

**Lotus Chinese Restaurant**
*Adjacent to the Caesar Hotel*
*Tel: 07-6376389*
A rich and varied Chinese menu, popular with reasonably priced business lunches. $$$

**The Blue Fish**
*Moriah Hotel*
*Coral Beach*
*Tel: 07-6337450*
Diverse selection of charcoal-grilled fish and seafood cooked in the French style. $$

# Nightlife

Nightlife in Israel is first and foremost an outdoor experience, meaning that visitors can simply enjoy themselves by strolling up and down the central streets of the main cities. Young and old flock to Jerusalem's Ben Yehuda and Salomon Street malls or Tel Aviv's Dizengoff Street or Schenkin Street to meander between streetside cafés, to see and be seen. These are ideal venues for finding a café table, ordering a coffee and cake, or perhaps a light meal and some wine, and watching the world go by. Even on weekday evenings such locations are very lively and should be avoided by those who dislike noise and crowds.

Israelis are not big consumers of alcohol. Nevertheless, the country has a lively pub scene. Jerusalem's Russian Compound is the capital's busiest drinking district but for all the carousing you will notice that most locals nurse one or two drinks through until the early hours. As elsewhere in the Mediterranean, there is a fine dividing line between a café and a bar and it is acceptable to sit drinking alcohol in a café or to go to a pub for a meal.

*Russian Compound busker*

Tourists, especially young singles, should bear in mind that hard-core nightlife in pubs, discos and nightclubs does not get going until after 11pm. Remember that the Israeli weekend comprises Friday and Saturday, so the busiest nights out are Thursday, Friday and Saturday nights.

For those who prefer a more sedate evening out at the theatre or a concert, Israel has much to offer, including world-class orchestras and dance companies. Visitors should try to take in a cultural performance either at the Sultan's Pool Amphitheatre in Jerusalem or the Caesarea Amphitheatre, both in superb settings – the former beneath the walls of the Old City (take some warm clothes even in summer) and the latter in a historical, Roman setting next to the Mediterranean. Schedules are available from ticket agents:

**Bimot**, 8 Shamai Street, Jerusalem, tel: 02-6250905/6.

**Rococo**, 93 Dizengoff Street, Tel Aviv, tel: 03-5226897.

## Theatre

Israelis are great theatre-goers but unfortunately most productions are in Hebrew, although simultaneous translations are sometimes provided and there are frequent performances by overseas companies, especially during the Israel Festival in May.

**JERUSALEM THEATRE**
*20 Marcus Street*
*Jerusalem*
*Tel: 02-5617167*

**HABIMAH THEATRE**
*Habimah Square*
*Tel Aviv*
*Tel: 03-6209888*

**HAIFA THEATRE**
*50 Pvazner Street*
*Haifa*
*Tel: 04-8620670*

## Music

**ISRAEL PHILHARMONIC ORCHESTRA**
*Mann Auditorium*
*11 Dizengoff Street/1 Huberman Street*
*Tel Aviv*
*Tel: 03-5289163*
Conducted by Zubin Mehta.

**NEW ISRAEL OPERA**
*28 Leonardo Da Vinci Street*
*Jerusalem*
*Tel: 03-6927707*
Also the home of the Rishon Le Zion Symphony Orchestra.

**THE JERUSALEM SYMPHONY ORCHESTRA**
*Henry Crown Hall, Jerusalem*
*Tel: 02-5617167*

**For jazz and folk music, try:**
**PARGOD THEATRE**
*94 Bezalel St, Jerusalem*
*Tel: 02-6231765*

**BET LESSING THEATRE**
*34 Weizman Boulevard*
*Tel Aviv*
*Tel: 03-6956222*

## Dance

Israel's two leading dance troupes, the Inbal Dance Theatre and the Batsheva Dance Theatre, both of which combine

***A night at the ballet***

oriental and Western dance movements in innovative routines, are based at the Suzan Dalal Centre in Tel Aviv's Neve Tsedek Quarter, tel: 03-5105656.

## Cinema

In addition to the latest Hollywood hits, Israeli cinemas also show the best movies from elsewhere in the world, usually with sub-titles in English, but ask at the box office to be sure. Check the *Jerusalem Post* for current showings. Each city has a cinemathèque which shows an eclectic range of fringe movies and golden oldies.

JERUSALEM CINEMATHEQUE
*Derekh Khevron*
*Tel: 02-6724131*

TEL AVIV CINEMATHEQUE
*2 Sprinza Street*
*Tel: 03-6917181*

HAIFA CINEMATHEQUE
*142 Ha-Nasi Boulevard*
*Tel: 04-8383424*

## Pubs

Pubs and bars are not an integral part of Israeli culture and most places are hang-outs for the young.

### Jerusalem

Popular watering holes in the Russian Compound include:

GLASNOST
*15 Heleni Ha-Malka Street*
*Tel: 02-6256954*

CASSO
*13 Monbaz Street*
*Tel: 02-6257078*

FINKS
*Corner of Ha-Histadrut and Ha-Melekh George*
*Tel: 02-6234523*

This popular spot tends to attract an older crowd.

### Tel Aviv

In Tel Aviv there is no specific bar district. The seafront promenade, Ha-Yarkon, Dizengoff, Schenkin, Florentin and Jaffa are all lively places to stop. Some recommended watering holes include:

MINISTRY OF SOUND
*2 Haim Vital Street*
*Florentin*
*Tel: 03-6815891*

LOT'S WIFE
*53 Arlozorov Street*
*Tel: 03-5235522*

HACOSIT
*5 Rabin Square*
*Tel: 03-5223244*

### Haifa

There is, inevitably, a pub district near the port as well as bars in midtown Hadar and uptown Central Carmel.

DALLAS
*30 Hanamal Street*
*Tel: 04-8676633*

THE GREEN BOTTLE
*72 Ha'atzmaut Street*
*Tel: 04-8673688*

***Jerusalem Underground disco***

*Open-air rock concert*

### Eilat

Eilat has lots of pubs just above the traffic-lights by the crossroads as the main desert highway reaches the sea. Recommended is:

GALLERIA
*Dekel Shopping Centre*
*Eilat*
*Tel: 07-9373655*

## Discos & Nightclubs

Once again, bear in mind that nightlife does not get going until after 11pm. If you arrive at a disco at 9pm you'll probably be the first person there. Jerusalem's nightclubs are concentrated in the Talpiot Commercial Centre south of the city, while Tel Aviv's Hamasger Street is the best place to head, though there are also many nightclubs with floor shows in Jaffa.

### Jerusalem

CANAAN
*8 Ha-Ta'asiyah Street*
*Talpiot*
*Jerusalem*
*Tel: 02-6735633*

HALLELUJAH
*Kibbutz Ramat Rachel*
*Jerusalem*
*Tel: 02-6736828*

### Tel Aviv

NOVEMBER
*15 Yefet Street*
*Jaffa*
*Tel: 03-6821243*

PORTO LOCO
*Yordei Ha-Sira Street*
*The Brazilian Club*
*Old Tel Aviv port*
*Tel: 03-5445224*

### Haifa

THE CHAPLAIN
*Dan Panorama Hotel*
*Ha-Nassi Boulevard*
*Haifa*
*Tel: 04-8252206*

### Eilat

GENESIS ROCK
*Paradise Hotel*
*Eilat*
*Tel: 07-9335050*

# Calendar of Special Events

The Jewish year follows a lunar-solar calendar with 12 lunar months a year plus a leap month every two to three years to bring the calendar in line with the solar year. This means Jewish festivals can vary by up to a month in the Gregorian calendar. Religious festivals aside, Israelis use the Gregorian calendar.

The Muslim calendar is completely lunar with 12 months a year. Festivals rotate backwards through the Gregorian calendar. Principal festivals are: New Year; Mohammed's Birthday; Ramadan (a month-long fast during the day with feasts after sunset); Id El Fitr (conclusion of Ramadan); and Id El Adha (Feast of the Sacrifice).

## JANUARY/FEBRUARY

**Orthodox Christmas**: The local Christian community is for the most part Orthodox and celebrates Christmas according to the Julian calendar on 6 January. The Armenian community celebrates Christmas on 14 January.

**Tu B'Shvat**: The Jewish New Year for trees is celebrated in late January or early February with tree-planting ceremonies around the country. For details phone the JNF Tree Planting Centre toll free: 177-022-3484.

*Purim party-goer*

## MARCH/APRIL

**Purim**: This festival held in March, has a carnival atmosphere and commemorates the deliverance of the Jews from terrible destruction in Persia. It is traditional for revellers to wear fancy dress and get drunk so as not to be able to distinguish good from evil.

*Passover supper*

**The Jerusalem International Book Festival**: Every alternate March at the Jerusalem International Congress Centre, tel: 02-6558558.

**Pesach** (Passover): Celebrated in late March or April. Recalls the exodus of the Jews from Egypt. During the week-long festival bread and yeast products are not eaten. The first and last days of Pesach are public holidays.

**Easter:** This falls on the weekend after the first day of Pesach because the

*Soldiers on Memorial Day*

Last Supper was the Pesach meal. The highlight is the Good Friday procession along the Via Dolorosa in Jerusalem.

**Holocaust Day:** In April (sometimes in early May). Commemorates the six million Jews who were killed by the Nazis. All places of entertainment are closed.

## MAY/JUNE

**Memorial Day**: Early May (sometimes late April). Commemorates members of Israeli forces who have died in defence of the country. All places of entertainment are closed.

**Independence Day**: Early May (sometimes late April). A public holiday celebrating Israel's independence in 1948. On the eve of the festival the city streets are packed with merrymakers hitting plastic hammers (of freedom) on the heads of passers-by.

**Lag B'Omer**: Held in May. An Israeli bonfire night celebrating a range of miracles and victories in battle.

**Shavuot** (Pentecost): In late May or early June. Commemorates the giving of the Torah to the Jews on Mount Sinai. It is also a harvest festival and public holiday.

**Israel Festival**: The country's biggest cultural event, including the best of Israeli and international drama, music and dance. For tickets contact the Jerusalem Theatre, tel: 02-2667167.

## JULY/AUGUST

The Jerusalem Film Festival in July shows films from around the world. Contact the Jerusalem Cinemathèque, tel: 02-6724936.

**Tisha B'Av**. Late July or early August. A traditional day of mourning and fasting commemorating the destruction of the Temple. All places of entertainment are closed.

**Tu B'Av:** In August. Marks the beginning of the grape harvest.

**Karmiel Dance Festival**: Galilee, in August, tel: 04-9987961 for details.

**Jaffa Nights**: A series of free outdoor concerts in August in Jaffa.

## SEPTEMBER/OCTOBER

**Rosh Ha'Shana**, the Jewish New Year: Early to mid-September. A 2-day public holiday.

**Yom Kippur**: The holiest day in the Jewish calendar, a 25-hour period of prayer and fasting to ask for forgiveness from God. Everything is closed and no public or private traffic is allowed on the roads.

**Succot** (Tabernacles): Commemorates the 40 years the Jews spent wandering in the desert. Families build small tabernacles and eat their meals inside. The first and last days of this 8-day festival are both public holidays. The last day, **Simchat Torah**, marks the beginning of the reading of a new Torah cycle.

**Akko Fringe Theatre Festival**: Held in Akko during Succot. Specialises in fringe productions. Tel toll free: 177-022-7764.

## NOVEMBER/DECEMBER

**Chanukah**: An 8-day festival of lights in which candles are lit to commemorate the re-dedication of the Temple after the victory over the Greeks. Gifts are given to children.

**Liturgica**: Held just before Christmas in December. This festival combines international and Israeli choirs.

**Christmas**: The highlight is Midnight Mass in Bethlehem's Manger Square.

# Practical Information

## GETTING THERE

### By Air

Almost all international flights land at Ben Gurion International Airport which is 19km (12 miles) southeast of Tel Aviv and 40km (25 miles) west of Jerusalem. There are some charter flights available direct to Eilat. El Al, Israel's national airline, all the major national airlines of Western Europe, and Air Canada, TWA and Delta have regular flights to Israel. There are many direct flights to Israel from 12 North American cities and El Al, British Airways and several charter companies fly to Israel from Heathrow, Gatwick, Stansted and Manchester in Great Britain. Flying time is four to five hours from Western Europe and 10 hours from the East Coast of the USA.

*Checking the route*

There is a Tourist Information Office at Ben Gurion Airport open round the clock, tel: 03-9712541

For flight information in English, tel: 03-9723344

### By Road

The borders with Lebanon and Syria are closed but there are three border crossings with Egypt and three more with Jordan. Cars are permitted to cross but are subject to long delays.

### Egypt

The border points at Rafah (Radiakh), southern tip of the Gaza Strip; Nitsana (Nizzana), Negev; and Taba, south of Eilat, are open every day of the year except Yom Kippur and Id El Adha. Rafah is open 8.30am–5pm. Nitsana – buses from Cairo to Tel Aviv and Jerusalem come via this crossing – is open 8am–4pm. Taba, mainly for travelling from the Sinai into Israel, is open 7am–9pm.

### Jordan

There are three border points. All are open Sunday to Thursday 8am–4pm, Friday 8am–11am.

The Arava checkpoint near Eilat, tel: 07-6336812. A bus service runs from Aqaba to Eilat.

The Jordan River Crossing near Beit

*Flowers flourish in the sun*

Shean, tel: 06-6586448. Served by buses from Amman.

The Allenby Bridge near Jericho, tel: 02-9941038. Served by buses from Amman and a taxi service to Jerusalem.

### By Sea

The Stability and Sol Lines offer regular sailings from Greece and Cyprus to Haifa.

## TRAVEL ESSENTIALS

### When to Visit

Many visitors want their vacation to coincide with religious festivals – in particular Passover and New Year for Jews, and Christmas and Easter for Christians. Remember that holy sites will be very crowded during these periods. From the point of view of climate, the early spring and autumn are the most pleasant times to visit Israel.

### Visas and Passports

Citizens of Western Europe, the USA, Canada and Australasia need only a valid passport. Visitors can remain in Israel for three months only, after which an extension visa must be acquired from the Ministry of the Interior.

For extensions apply to:

**Ministry of the Interior**, 1 Shlomzion Hamalkah Street, Jerusalem, tel: 02-6290222.

**Shalom Tower**, Visa Dept., 9 Ahad Haíam Street, Tel Aviv, tel: 03-5193333.

### Vaccinations

No vaccinations are required for entry to Israel.

### Customs

European Union-style red (goods to declare) and green (no goods to declare) channels operate in Israel. Duty-free allowances per adult include 250 cigarettes or 250 grams of tobacco, 1 litre of spirits, 2 litres of wine, 0.25 litres of perfume, and gifts not exceeding $200 (about £135). Expensive items such as cameras, jewellery and electronic equipment may be taken into Israel providing they are taken out again. In theory, the authorities can ask for a deposit but are only likely to do so in the case of bulky and very expensive electronic goods.

### Weather

Israeli summers are long, dry and hot with average temperatures of 30°C (86°F) An oppressively hot sun shines from May to September. The Mediterranean coast is very humid but Jerusalem has a drier climate and cool evening breezes. Winters are wet and mild with 600mm (24 inches) of rain falling between November and March. Average temperatures are 18°C (64°F) in Tel Aviv and a cool 11°C (52°F) in Jerusalem which is in the mountains. Eilat and the Dead Sea are ideal winter vacation spots with average winter temperatures of 21°C (70°F).

### Clothing

Dress in Israel is very informal but remember to dress modestly (women covering arms and legs) for visiting holy sites. Indeed, keeping as much of the body covered as possible is a good idea for protection against the sun. Remember to bring a large-brimmed hat. In the summer bring plenty of open-neck shirts, shorts, light trousers and cotton dresses as well as beachwear and swimsuits. Avoid heavy materials such as denim jeans. In Jerusalem, a light sweater or jacket is needed for the evenings. In the winter, warm coats, heavy sweaters, raincoats and jackets are also needed but bring summery clothes too because the weather between October and April can be very changeable.

*Protective sun hat*

### Electricity

220 volts AC.

### Time Differences

Israel is two hours ahead of Greenwich Mean Time and seven hours ahead of US Eastern Time. Summer time is imposed from late March to September.

## GETTING ACQUAINTED

### Geography

Israel is located at the eastern tip of Asia and bordering Africa and Europe. A small country, 21,000 sq. km (8,108 sq. miles) in size, including the Palestinian autonomous territories, it is divided into three distinct geographical regions running from north to south – the Mediterranean Coast, the inland hills, and the Syrian-African rift valley, which includes the River Jordan, the Dead Sea and the Red Sea.

### Government

Israel is a democracy with elections at least every four years for a 120-seat single chamber parliament called the Knesset. A system of proportional representation means that the Knesset is fragmented between many parties. The prime minister is directly chosen by a separate ballot concurrent with Knesset elections. The president, the titular head of state like the British monarch, is chosen every 5 years by a secret ballot of Knesset members.

### Economy

Rapid economic growth during the early 1990s due to mass immigration, development of a flourishing high-tech sector and the peace process saw living standards in Israel rise to a level comparable to Britain or Italy. The country exports goods valued at more than US $20 billion every year, of which 60 percent have high-tech components.

*A devout worshipper*

### Religion

Though Israel is nominally a Jewish state, most Israelis are not orthodox Jews. Some 20 percent of Jews are orthodox, with the remaining 80 percent ranging from traditional to stridently secular and campaigning for separation of synagogue and state. About 17.5 percent of Israelis are Muslims, 2 percent are Christians and 1.5 percent are Druze. Most of the Palestinians in the West Bank and Gaza are Muslims though there is a Christian minority of several percent.

### How Not To Offend

Israelis value candour and will often surprise you by their bluntness and openness. That said, you should remember religious sensitivities and dress and behave modestly at the holy sites in orthodox Jewish neighbourhoods and Arab towns. Venturing unsolicited political opinions about the Israel–Arab conflict can also cause offence but if asked feel free to be frank.

### Population

Israel has a population of nearly 6 million including a 20 percent Arab minority. The Jewish majority includes over 700,000 new immigrants from the former Soviet Union who have reached Israel since 1990, as well as large communities originating in North Africa, Yemen, Iraq, Persia, Poland, Hungary, Romania, Bulgaria, Ethiopia, Argentina and the USA. In addition, there are over 2 million Palestinians living in the West Bank and Gaza.

## MONEY MATTERS

### Currency

The Israeli currency is the New Israel Shekel (NIS) which is divided into 100 agorot. Notes are issued in four denominations: 20 NIS (grey with a portrait of former prime minister Moshe Sharett); 50 NIS (purple with a portrait of the Nobel Prize Winner for Literature, Shai Agnon); 100 NIS (light grey with a portrait of former president Yitzhak Ben Zvi); 200 NIS (reddish-brown with a portrait of former president Zalman Shazar). Small change comes in coins of 5 agorot, 10 agorot and half a shekel (brass), and 1

*Cash on demand*

shekel, 5 shekels and 10 shekels (silver).

The NIS is relatively stable and floats freely on the world's currency markets with a daily revised exchange rate according to supply and demand. All banks offers similar exchange rates, as do *bureaux de change* and money changers (though the latter two charge less commission than banks).

Unlimited amounts of foreign currency can be taken into Israel but only $10,000 (about £6,500) taken out unless larger amounts have been registered at the port of entry. Only a maximum of $500 (about £330) worth of shekels can be converted back to foreign currency and only $100 (about £65) at the airport, so it is advisable not to over-convert in the first place. Most vendors will accept dollars and other major currencies but will offer an inferior exchange rate.

### Credit Cards & Traveller's Cheques

All the major credit cards (Visa, Eurocard/Mastercard, American Express and Diners Club) are honoured in Israel and most stores, restaurants, hotels and other vendors and even museums are happy to accept them. In the event of loss see *Useful Addresses*.

Traveller's cheques are accepted by all banks but incur very high commission charges. There is a percentage charge on each traveller's cheque so higher denomination cheques are more cost-efficient.

### Cash Machines

There are countless cash dispensing machines that accept international credit cards. Do not be put off by the Hebrew instructions on the screen. As soon as you enter your card the instructions will switch to English.

### Tipping

Tips of 10–15 percent are expected at restaurants and cafés though not if service is included in the bill. Hotel porters, chambermaids and hairdressers all expect small tips. Taxi drivers are not tipped by Israelis but expect to be tipped by tourists. Try to be discriminating, rewarding good service.

### Taxes

VAT amounts to 17 percent but is not applicable in hotels or for car hire if payment is made by foreign currency. Eilat is a VAT-free zone.

### Money Changers

Officially the money changers in East Jerusalem are illegal but they are allowed to function in an institutional manner. They offer similar rates to the banks but save queuing and avoid the bureaucracy of banks.

## GETTING AROUND

### Taxis

Taxis come in all shapes and sizes and are marked in green along the side and on top. Most drivers speak some English. In town insist that the driver runs the meter and for longer journeys agree a fare in advance. Ask for inter-city tariffs at your hotel. Taxis can be hailed in the street or ordered by phone.

*Taxi!*

*Deserted night-time station*

### Air

Though Israel is a small country there are regular, reasonably priced air services which save time if travelling to the Galilee or Eilat and offer stunning views of the country. Phone Arkia Airlines for details, tel: 02-6255888.

### Sheruts

These are shared taxis that travel fixed routes, both between the major cities and along bus routes within cities. Fares are similar to those on buses. *Sheruts* are especially useful on Friday night/Saturday when there is no public transport.

### Buses

The bus is the essential form of public transport in Israel. The Egged national bus company runs a punctual, efficient service which despite steep fare increases in recent years is still reasonably priced. Beware though: bus drivers go too fast and have a habit of leaving 30 seconds before the advertised time. There are no buses on Friday evening/Saturday except in Haifa and Eilat. Students, children (5–18) and pensioners get a 5 percent discount. Children under the age of 5 go free. There are worthwhile weekly and monthly ride-as-much-as-you-want tickets.
Egged information:
**Jerusalem**, tel: 02-5304555
**Tel Aviv**, tel: 03-5375555

### Trains

Despite attempts to expand the system, Israel's trains are under-used. There is a good service between Tel Aviv and Haifa but the Tel Aviv–Jerusalem line, which winds through the hills, though good for sightseeing, takes 2 hours – the bus takes 45-minutes. There are no trains on Friday evening/Saturday. Fares are cheaper than on buses, and students and pensioners get 25 percent discount.
**Information**, tel: 03-6937515

### Metro

Haifa has a subway called the Carmelit. This six-station system, which is really an underground cable car, offers the fastest way of moving from downtown to mid-town to uptown Haifa.

### Car

Israel has a well-developed road system which for much of the time is jammed up, especially in the Tel Aviv and Jerusalem regions. As in other Mediterranean societies, drivers are fast and dangerous, weaving in and out of traffic and continually honking the horn.

Car hire is expensive if arranged in Israel but a lot cheaper if booked before embarking on your visit. The biggest local company is Eldan. Hertz, Avis, Eurocar and others all have offices at Ben Gurion Airport.

### Hitchhiking

This is a national institution and there are hitchhiking stations at all major junctions. This can be an effective way of travelling around the more remote regions of the Negev and Galilee but there are often long lines of other hikers, including soldiers who get priority.

## HOURS AND HOLIDAYS

### Business Hours

Most businesses operate Sunday to Thursday 8am–4pm. Stores usually stay open until 7pm or even later and are often also open on Friday morning and Saturday night. Banks open Sunday to Thursday 8.30am–12.30pm and on Friday 8.30am–noon, as well as Sunday, Tuesday and Thursday afternoon from 4–5.30pm.

### Public Holidays

Everything closes down for the Sabbath from Friday afternoon until an hour after sunset on Saturday. Similarly all public holidays/festivals last from sunset to sunset. Public holidays when businesses are closed are: Rosh Hashanah (Jewish New Year) in September; Yom Kippur (Day of Atonement) in September/October; Succot (Tabernacles: first and last days are public holidays) in September/October; Pesach (Passover: first and last days) in March/April; Yom Haíatzmaut (Independence Day) in April/May; Shavuot (Pentecost) in May/June.

## HEALTH AND EMERGENCIES

### General Health

Tap water is drinkable in Israel and there is plenty of mineral water available. Generally speaking, Western levels of hygiene apply. Aids, as elsewhere, is a problem, though levels of infection are lower than in the West.

By far the biggest health problem for visitors relates to the sun and heat: tourists tend to behave irresponsibly, either sightseeing without drinking enough water or sunbathing for hours on end. The symptoms of dehydration include headaches, stomach upset, fever and diarrhoea, so visitors often mistake dehydration for a foreign bug. Drink at least half a litre an hour when it is very hot.

### Pharmacies

Most pharmacists speak English and are very helpful. The *Jerusalem Post* will list duty pharmacies which open at nights and weekends.

### Medical Care

Israel has the largest proportion of doctors per head of the population anywhere in the world. This is no comfort if you feel ill, and inevitably extensive medical care is very expensive, so make sure you have insurance. Doctors will charge about $40 (about £25) for a consultation and hospitals will accept emergencies. In emergency wards, patients are treated according to the extent of their pain so do not be stoically silent.

For an ambulance or information about duty hospitals, tel: 101.

There are bound to be dozens of English-speaking dentists near your hotel. Ask at reception for a recommendation.

### Crime/Trouble

Theft is rampant in Israel so keep a close eye on belongings, but violent crime is very rare. Most violent incidents are linked to the security situation so consult your hotel reception before travelling to the West Bank or Gaza (though media coverage tends to exaggerate the dangers).

Illegal drugs such as hashish and heroin (usually grown in neighbouring Lebanon) are easily available in Israel. Prosecutions are not often brought against hashish users but in any event visitors are likely to find themselves deported rather than prosecuted. Heroin is taken more seriously.

Prostitution is legal in Israel and although homosexuality is illegal no prosecution has ever been brought against consenting adults.

### Police

The police can be helpful, especially the tourist police (Jerusalem, tel: 02-6273222; Tel Aviv, tel: 03-5454444) who are meant to protect visitors from being ripped off. Israelis themselves (perhaps because so many do reserve duty in the army) tend not to obey the police and the sight of an irate citizen arguing with an exasperated policeman is common. Most police speak some English, and if you are in trouble most soldiers will be happy to help you too. The traffic police tend to be lenient with tourists.

**Police emergency**, tel: 100

### Toilets

Public toilets are few and far between though they are usually found in popular tourist spots. Otherwise nip into a hotel or a hamburger joint.

## COMMUNICATIONS AND NEWS

### Post

The Israel Postal Authority has over 700 branches, displaying the symbol of a white stag on a red background. They sell stamps and phone cards and offer express and regular mail services, fax and telegram services, and exchange Girocheques and Eurocheques and effect Western Union cash transfers. Post boxes are yellow for in-town mail and red for out of town and abroad. Main branches are open from 8am–8pm,

*Colour-coded post boxes*

*Catching up on the news*

and agencies from 8am–1pm and 4–7pm. Mail to Europe and America takes less than a week.

Kiosks and stores also sell stamps and phone cards.

For toll-free information about the post office, tel: 177-022-2121.

### Telephone

Phones are operated by cards, coins or credit cards. Israel's international dialling code is **972** and the country is divided into the following area codes: 02-Jerusalem; 03-Tel Aviv; 04-Haifa; 06-North; 07-South; 08- South Central; 09-North Central; 050 Pelephone (mobile); 052 Cellcom (mobile).

Mobile phones are popular and can be hired quite cheaply by the day.

Domestic calls are cheapest from 8pm–8am and Friday afternoons and Saturdays. They are most expensive from 8am–1pm (Sunday to Friday).

International calls (except to North America) are most expensive from 8am–10pm. There is a 25 percent reduced tariff from 10pm–1am and all day Saturday and Sunday, and a 40 percent reduction from 1am–8am. Calls to North America are most expensive from 1pm–midnight with a 25 percent reduction from 8am–1pm and at weekends, and a 40 percent reduction from midnight to 8am. To ring abroad, dial 00, then 1 for Canada and the US, 44 for the UK, 61 for Australia, 64 for New Zealand and 353 for Ireland.

Overseas reverse charge (collect) calls can be made by dialling the international operator on 188. There are toll free numbers (beginning with 177) to connect with an operator abroad for such calls or for debiting a credit card or subscriber account.

**UK** (British Telecom) 177-440-2727
**USA** (A.T&T) 177-100-2727
**USA** (Sprint) 177-102-2727
**USA** (MCI) 177-150-2727
**Canada** 177-105-2727

### Useful numbers

**Police**: 100
**Ambulance**: 101
**Fire services**: 102
**Internet services**: 135
**Reverse charge calls**: 142
**Directory enquiries**: 144

## MEDIA

### Newspapers

Visitors can keep astride local matters with the *Jerusalem Post*, which also offers useful listings for local cinemas, TV programmes, religious services, museums and duty pharmacies. The bi-weekly *Jerusalem Report* is also worth reading. In addition there are daily newspapers in Hebrew, Arabic and Russian

### TV & Radio

In addition to two state-owned channels and one commercial station, Israelis receive some 50 channels on cable TV including BBC, CNN and Sky News. Israel's Channel One has a daily English-language news broadcast at 6.15pm. Both Lebanon and Jordan have an English-language TV station.

Israel Radio broadcasts on six channels, including English-language news programmes on Reshet Aleph at 7am, 1pm. and 5pm. The BBC World Service and Voice of America can be picked up clearly.

## ACCOMMODATION

Israel has over 300 hotels ranging from the luxurious and very expensive through to budget-priced accommodation. In addition, there are numerous youth hostels and B&B-style guest houses. Two uniquely Israeli types of accommodation are kibbutz guest houses and Christian hospices. Though these sound austere, they are in fact comfortable places to stay and every bit as expensive as good quality hotels.

Kibbutz Guest Houses, Head Office, 90 Rehov Ben Yehuda, Tel Aviv, tel: 03-5243358.

The following categories are based on guests turning up on spec to stay overnight; package-tour prices are often much lower, less than half price.

$$$=expensive; $$=moderate; $=inexpensive.

### *Jerusalem*

**KING DAVID HOTEL**
*23 King David Street (David Ha-Melekh)*
*Tel: 02-6208888*
*Fax: 02-6232303*
The country's leading hotel, sought after for its old-world ambience and splendid

gardens overlooking the Old City. World leaders and the rich and famous stay here – perhaps because of this service verges on the complacent. $$$

**LAROMME HOTEL**
*3 Jabotinski Street*
*Tel: 02-6756666*
*Fax: 02-6756777*
Excellent service and stylish location has made this hotel a worthy rival of the King David. $$$

**AMERICAN COLONY HOTEL**
*Derekh Shkem*
*Tel: 02-6285171*
*Fax: 02-6279779*
The city's oldest hotel. Favoured by the foreign press corps because of its location between West and East Jerusalem. $$

**MITZPEH RACHEL**
*Kibbutz Ramat Rachel*
*Tel: 02-6702555*
*Fax: 02-6733155*
Within Jerusalem's city limits with a splendid panorama of the Judean desert. $$

**OUR SISTERS OF ZION**
*Ein Kerem*
*Tel: 02-6415738*
Delightful Provence-style pension in Ein Kerem with spacious gardens filled with lemon and olive trees tended by the nuns. $$

**NEVE ILAN**
*D.N. Hare Yehuda (near Jerusalem)*
*Tel: 02-5348111*
*Fax: 02-5348197*
Pleasant hillside country club atmosphere with a commanding view of the coastal plain. Just 20 minutes away from Jerusalem. $$

**RON HOTEL**
*Zion Square (Kikar Tsiyon)*
*Tel: 02-6253471*
*Fax: 02-6250707*
Located in the heart of West Jerusalem, this hotel has the charm of a Central European pension. $

***Jerusalem luxury***

### Tel Aviv

**Tel Aviv Hilton**
*Independence Park*
*Tel: 03-5202222*
*Fax: 03-5272711*
Overlooking the sea-front promenade and park; this is the city's most expensive and fashionable hotel. **$$$**.

**Adiv Hotel**
*5 Mendele Street*
*Tel: 03-5229141*
*Fax: 03-5229144*
Friendly, comfortable and convenient. Over the road from the beach with view of the sea and a good quality, moderately priced self-service cafeteria. **$$**

**Shfayim Kibbutz Guest House**
*Kibbutz Shfayim*
*Tel: 09-9523434*
Situated close to the Mediterranean coast, only and a short ride from Tel Aviv. **$$**.

**Deborah Hotel**
*87 Ben Yehuda Street*
*Tel: 03-5278282*
In a quiet location north of the city, and about five minutes from the beach. **$**

### Haifa and the North

**Dan Carmel**
*85–7 Ha-Nasi Boulevard*
*Haifa*
*Tel: 04-8306211*
*Fax: 04-8387504*
The city's most stylish hotel, on the summit of Mount Carmel and commanding a splendid panorama of the bay. **$$$**

**Rimon Inn**
*Artists Quarter*
*Safed*
*Tel: 06-6920655*

***Hyatt Hotel***

*Fax: 06-6920456*
*Toll free 177-022-7676*
Homely hotel, charmingly located in the alleyways of Safed with wonderful views of the Galilee hills. **$$$**

**Galei Kinneret**
*1 Eliezer Kaplan Street*
*Tiberias*
*Tel: 06-6728888*
*Fax: 06-6790260*
*Toll free 177-022-8686*
On the lakeside in Tiberias, this is one of the city's oldest hotels. **$$**

**Kfar Blum Guest House**
*Kibbutz Kfar Blum*
*Tel: 06-6948511*
*Fax: 06-6948555*
Overlooked by the snow-capped Mount Hermon to the east, the River Jordan flows through this kibbutz. **$**

**Central Hotel**
*37 Rehov Yerushalayim*
*Safed*
*Tel: 06-6972666*
In the heart of Safed by the ancient synagogue neighbourhood, this makes a good base for seeing the Galilee. **$**

### Eilat and the Dead Sea

**Royal Beach**
*North Beach*
*Eilat*
*Tel: 07-6368888*
*Fax: 07-6368811*
A large hotel with an exotic array of swimming pools and restaurants overlooking the beach and the lagoona. **$$$**

**Dead Sea Hyatt Regency**
*Ein Bokek*
*Tel: 07-6591234*
*Fax: 07-6591235*
The newest and most luxurious hotel by the Dead Sea. **$$$**

**Lagoona**
*North Beach*
*Eilat*
*Tel: 07-6366666*
*Fax: 07-6332089*
Stylish, overlooking the lagoona. **$$**

ETZION HOTEL
*Tel: 07-6370003*
Far from the beach but next to the Central Bus Station. $

## Bed & Breakfast

There is a very limited amount of B&B accommodation in Israel, though both Jerusalem and the Galilee do have some choice. In Jerusalem there is a B&B central information office called **Good Morning Jerusalem** at the International Congress Centre near the Central Bus Station, tel: 02-6511270.

In the Galilee try the vegetarian village of Amirim which also offers superb views of the region, tel: 06-6989572; fax: 06-6980772.

# USEFUL INFORMATION

## Disabled

Visitors in need of wheelchairs, oxygen tanks and related equipment can contact: Yad Sarah, 43 Haneviim Street, Jerusalem, tel: 02-6244242; fax: 02-6244493. Book at least two weeks before your visit.

## Children

Israelis love to indulge children so there is no need to keep apologising for noise and mess. Restaurants, beyond the junk food chains, rarely have a children's menu but will be pleased to cater for children's fussy eating habits. Children under 4 must be strapped into special seats in cars (except taxis), and children under 5 travel free on the buses.

## Language

Israelis are very adept at languages and almost everybody speaks some English. Hebrew and Arabic are the official languages but you will also hear Russian, French, Spanish, Yiddish and a dozen other languages.

## Useful Addresses

### Tourist Information Offices:

**Jerusalem**
17 Jaffa Street tel: 02-6258844
Jaffa Gate, tel: 02-6280382
**Tel Aviv**
New Central Bus Station, tel: 03-6395660
**Eilat**
Yotam Street (corner of Ha'arava Street), tel: 07-6372111
**Nazareth**
Casa Nova Street, tel: 06-6573003

### Tourist Offices Overseas:

**Canada**
Suite 700, 180 Bloor Street West, Toronto, Ontario, tel: 416-964-3784
**USA**
350 Fifth Avenue, 19th Floor, NY, tel: 212-560-0650
**UK**
18 Great Marlborough Street, London W1V 1AF, tel: 0171-464 3651

## Embassies in Israel

**Australia**
37 Shaul Hamelekh Boulevard, Tel Aviv, tel: 03-6950451
**Canada**
220 Hayarkon Street, Tel Aviv, tel: 03-5272929
**UK**
192 Hayarkon Street, Tel Aviv, tel: 03-5249171
**US**
71 Hayarkon Street, Tel Aviv, tel: 03-5174338

## Useful Internet Sites

Israel's Foreign Ministry (for general information about Israel), url:http//www-mfa.gov.il.

Ministry of Tourism- http://www.israel-mfa.gov.il/gov/tourism!.htmi

## Further Reading

Two full-size Insight Guides – one to Israel and one to Jerusalem – provide in-depth cultural coverage and top photography. Two Insight Compact Guides on the same destinations are fact-packed mini-encyclopedias.

***Children will be indulged***

# Index

## M



## N



## P, Q, R



## S

# ACKNOWLEDGMENTS


*Photography by*

| | |
|---|---|
| *2/3, 10, 13T, 14, 15, 16, 20, 21, 23, 24, 25, 26, 27, 28, 29, 30, 31B, 32, 33, 34, 35, 36, 37, 38, 39, 40, 41, 43, 44, 45, 46B, 47, 48, 49, 50, 51, 52, 53, 55, 56, 57, 58, 61, 62, 64, 65, 66T, 67, 68, 70, 71, 72, 73, 74, 75, 76, 77, 78, 79, 80, 81, 82, 83, 84, 85, 86, 87, 88, 89, 90, 91* | Richard Nowitz |
| *46T* | Sammy Avnisan |
| *13, 22, 31T, 59, 63, 66B* | Gary-John Norman |
| *69* | Axel Krause |
| *Cover* | Richard Nowitz |

| | |
|---|---|
| *Managing Editor* | Dorothy Stannard |
| *Production Editor* | Mohammed Dar |
| *Handwriting* | V Barl |
| *Designer* | Graham Mitchener |
| *Cover Design* | Klaus Geisler |
| *Cartography* | Berndtson & Berndtson |